ON THE BORDER OF WAR AND PEACE

POLISH INTELLIGENCE AND DIPLOMACY IN
1937–1939
AND THE ORIGINS OF THE ULTRA SECRET

RICHARD A. WOYTAK

EAST EUROPEAN QUARTERLY, BOULDER
DISTRIBUTED BY COLUMBIA UNIVERSITY PRESS
NEW YORK

1979

EAST EUROPEAN MONOGRAPHS, NO. XLIX

TO
LW

ACKNOWLEDGMENTS

It is always a pleasure to write acknowledgments. The author expresses his thanks and gratitude above all to his teachers at the University of California, Santa Barbara, in particular to Professor Dimitrije Djordjevic. A special debt of gratitude belongs to Professor Wacław Jędrzejewicz of the Piłsudski Institute in New York City, whose advice greatly facilitated my labors over the years. My appreciation is extended to Professor Anna Cienciala, who read my manuscript and unselfishly gave her time and attention. Special thanks are given to the Kościuszko Foundation, New York City, for its contribution. I am most grateful to all the individuals in England, Poland, and the United States who have helped make this book possible.

Richard A. Woytak
Carmel, California
December, 1977

MAPS

I. Map of Teschen (Cieszyn) Silesia showing the Jabłonków Tunnel is reproduced from B. Kożusznik's *The Problem of Cieszyn Silesia* (London, 1943). p. 24.

II. Map illustrating the German Memorandum presented at Godesberg, September 23, 1938; showing the Oderberg (Bohumin, Bogumin) Junction and City to be ceded to Germany. *DGFP*, Series D, Vol. II, Document 585.

TABLE OF CONTENTS

INTRODUCTION

No nation in modern history has experienced more territorial change than has Poland. In the 18th century, this state was one of the largest land domains in Europe. Yet, in a very short period, by a few distinct partitions, it disappeared for over a hundred years. The grief, shock, or neurosis of the Polish nation caused by the loss of its statehood and possession of a continuous area of space was to play an inordinate role in Polish history. For almost every 20 years up to 1863, then 1905, the Poles revolted in a series of insurrections demanding liberty and territorial space. These revolts were crushed. Nevertheless, the national aspirations of the Poles were not quenched. The Poles clandestinely plotted, intrigued, and were in the forefront of most European revolutionary movements of the 19th and early 20th centuries.

The dream of every Polish patriot was national independence and, with it, territorial irredenta however large or small. Their literature, art, geography, and history continually dealt with this subject. Polish poets appealed to God to bring a "Great War" to the partitioning powers, and at the outset of the year 1918 it seemed their prayers were heard at last. The "Black Eagles" of Russia, Austria and Prussian Germany were being destroyed or partitioned. Poland, the country of the white eagle, emerged violently from this cataclysm. In such a way, the galvanizing idea of territorial and national homogeneity was realized in post-World War I Europe. However, in contrast to historical claims, the idea of national and territorial homogeneity had to be militarily fought out, especially in East Central Europe.

A series of territorial struggles erupted in Posnania, Silesia, and Danzig against Germany. In the south a conflict broke out between Poles and Czechs for the Duchy of Teschen. In the east the Poles fought against Ukrainian, Lithuanian, White, and Red Russian forces. In this manner, the new frontiers of Poland were established by force of Polish arms and not by the Treaty of Versailles. This treaty accepted Poland's western frontiers as it recognized the new borders all over Europe.

Nevertheless, Poland's borders were not secure, for about one million Germans were left in Poland and about two million Poles in Germany. Poland's eastern borderlands were inhabited by a majority of non-Poles. From the historical experience of partition and the regaining of independence, Poland was very much concerned with securing her newly-fought-over frontiers. To the leaders of the nation, any territorial concessions or change in the west or in the east was considered equivalent to the establishment of foreign domination. During the inter-war years, 1918-1939, the main task of Polish leadership and diplomacy was to prevent this occurrence. These men who boldly led the state considered themselves a chosen generation, for they brought into reality·a reborn Poland that had been only a dream of their fathers and grandfathers.

The major Polish figure to emerge out of World War I was Józef Piłsudski. He was a modern socialist-nationalist combined with an age-old gentry freedom fighter and dedicated, as Garibaldi was in Italy in the 1860s to a resurrected Poland. Piłsudski's program, which called for an independent nation, was looked upon by many as a chimerical or romantic dream. Nevertheless, his efforts and those of other Poles, combined with the unpredictable outcome of the war, created the fulfillment of the dream. His personality dominated the government's main policy: the maintenance of national independence so dearly fought for and won.

Following Poland's success in the 1919-1920 Russo-Polish war, Marshal Piłsudski-whose prior leadership experience had been limited to clandestine and military operations-realized that the struggles for the frontiers were temporarily ending, and a new phase in Poland's development must begin. He promoted the consolidation of peace, so that the war-ravaged state could strengthen itself socially, politically, and economically. Piłsudski did not look with favor on normal political disharmony, judging it a luxury not yet affordable by Poland. In 1926 the old marshal staged a successful coup and set up a semi-dictatorship. He was affectionately called *dziadek* (grandfather) by the bulk of the Polish people. With his death in 1935, Piłsudski left a void that was never completely filled. Thus, his ghost still ruled Poland till 1939.

The men that followed him had been his soldiers, and like Piłsudski, were dedicated to the cause of an independent Poland. Piłsudski's foreign policy was inherited by Józef Beck, whose training was acquired under the direct influence of the late marshal. Beck absorbed many of Piłsudski's convictions, notably that one must be constantly vigilant in protecting Polish freedom and territorial integrity, and that it was the new government's duty to offset any moves which might conceivably prove to Poland's disadvantage. Being a soldier, Beck directed Poland's course along the lines of a military strategist, who envisaged for each independent move forward two or more channels for retreat and who-at the same time-was on the lookout against an outflanking movement. Hence, Beck constantly walked the lonely "tight-rope" in an effort to maintain the delicate balance between the forces on Poland's eastern and western frontiers. However, with the rise of the dynamic ideologies of communism and fascism led by Russia and Germany, the effort was becoming more complicated and difficult.

The Poles had two formal non-aggression pacts, one signed with the Soviets in 1932 and the other with Hitler's Germany in 1934. Hitler hoped that his pact with Piłsudski would bring about a reversal in Polish-German relations and that the two nations would march together against the east. Almost from the moment of the signing of the Berlin-Warsaw non-aggression agreement the Germans put out feelers for closer military cooperation with the Poles. In 1936 they offered to rearm the Polish army, navy, and air force with the latest German weapons. This offer was rejected.[1] In contrast to the West, where Germany represented a limited danger, the Russian threat with its communist ideology constituted an unlimited menace. The Poles considered any closer contact beyond the non-aggression pact with Soviet Russia to be most dangerous to Poland's independence. On the other hand, the Poles hoped to build and maintain a neutral corridor from Scandinavia to the Black Sea, a "Third Europe" between Germany and Russia-for an alliance or a war between the two would prove disastrous for Poland. In this manner, the Poles hoped to stay clear of any close understandings. Their policy was militarily defensive.

A natural outgrowth of this policy was the need to know as much as possible about the intentions of Poland's eastern and western neighbors. Although a relatively poor country, Poland was forced to spend a great deal of its national wealth on military arms. A sizable part of this expenditure went to the military intelligence department, *Oddział II* (Second Department), the major center for gathering information on Russia and Germany. In contrast to many other countries, Polish intelligence was organized in one central military institution, and it included both internal and external intelligence. This intelligence organ reported jointly to the military and government. *Oddział II* also engaged in counter-intelligence. Its personnel consisted of approximately 800 officers and military non-commissioned functionaries, not including civilian workers and agents in the field. Its internal organizational working structure was complicated. The chief of *Oddział II*, who had direct access to the army chief-of-staff, had two departments working under his command. One concentrated on gathering information from its military attachés in foreign countries. These attachés had, in turn, semi-independent small organizations under their control and command. A second research organization was divided into three research centers: the west "Germany," east "Russia," and a "General Studies" section, which included schooling, organization and budget, an intelligence library, and a drafting bureau. These three centers were divided into "shallow" frontier intelligence activity directed against Germany. They were located in the cities of Bydgoszcz (Station No. 3) and in Katowice (Station No. 4), covering the western border regions, East Prussia, Danzig, and the terrain east of the Oder River. The Łódź (Station No. 6) was being organized in 1938-1939; it did not function as a normal intelligence section. The "deep" intelligence activity was based on the consulate network within Germany and in adjacent countries. This network also had agents working beyond direct Warsaw intelligence control. Funds for these operations were supplied through normal diplomatic channels or were deposited in special bank accounts in Spain, Portugal, and Switzerland. The east "shallow" service was directed by the two centers in the cities of Wilno (Station No. 1) and Lwów (Station No. 5) and also a border defense corps which supplemented intelligence gathering. The "deep" penetration of Soviet Russia was controlled directly by the Second Department of the Polish General Staff located in Warsaw. The General Studies Section also had two centers: a Third Department for military planning for Russia and Germany including radio intelligence, counter-intelligence and codes, plus an independent organ directly reporting to the intelligence chief of *Ekspozytura* (Station No. 2). This station concentrated on diversion, sabotage, and propaganda with sections for Germany, Russia, Danzig, Czechoslovakia, and Lithuania. Polish counter-intelligence covered all the above sections, departments and stations.

In the late 1930s, an appeasement climate conditioned by political and military circles saw the rise of German territorial demands and national dynamism which resulted in the increase of international tensions, culminating in Hitler's desire for *Anschluss* with Austria in 1938.

By using sources that in the most part are new, this study intends to disclose how an economically backward but proud nation, placed in the unenviable geographical position between Germany and Russia, tried to resolve such a predicament and maintain her integrity.

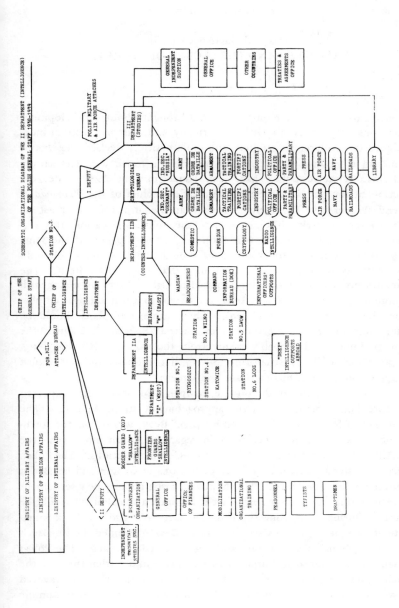

SCHEMATIC ORGANIZATIONAL DIAGRAM OF THE II DEPARTMENT (INTELLIGENCE)
OF THE POLISH GENERAL STAFF 1938-1939

Schematic Organizational Diagram of the Second Department (Intelligence) of the Polish General Staff 1938-1939

CHAPTER ONE

THE AUSTRIAN CRISIS:
FALL OTTO AND THE SECRET OF SECRETS

Events during the first months of 1938 brought about a development of tensions between Adolf Hitler's Germany and Austria. Austrian independence ran counter to publicly and diplomatically declared designs of uniting all German-speaking peoples outside the Reich with Germany.[1] A German strategic policy had been issued in June 1937 under the direction of the war minister and commander-in-chief of the *Wehrmacht*, General Werner von Blomberg, stating that the armed forces must be ready to repel attack, although, due to the political situation, this was considered unlikely. General von Blomberg's policy paper, at the same time, pointed out that the *Wehrmacht* should "be able to exploit militarily any favorable political opportunity that might offer itself." The German army was advised to be prepared to fight a "two-front war with the emphasis in the West (Case Red), and a two-front war with the emphasis in the Southeast (Case Green)." Three other war plans should be made: German armed intervention in Austria (Special Case Otto: the cryptogrammic word probably comes from the name of Otto Habsburg, the pretender to the Austrian throne); conflict in Spain; and war against Britain, Poland, and Lithuania (Case Red/Green).[2]

Berlin, in an extended diplomatic campaign of assurances, expected to secure Polish neutrality in the approaching Austrian *Anschluss*. The aim of Polish foreign policy, guided by Józef Beck, was to use the forthcoming crisis to secure concessions in regard to Polish interests in the Free City of Danzig and to stabilize Polish-German relations.[3] The Polish foreign minister's visit to the League of Nations in Geneva and his Berlin stopover on January 13-14, 1938, hoped to bring about a new settlement between Berlin and Warsaw. Beck let it be known that Poland would be neutral.[4] During their conversations, the Germans also let Beck know of their designs against Czechoslovakia. Beck described Polish-Czech relations as being in a bad state and not expected to change. The Polish foreign minister hoped to initiate a new fundamental settlement over the Danzig question and other matters. Hitler indicated that he favored the status quo in relations between Germany and Poland. In world public opinion, on the eve of the Austrian takeover, both nations maintained an atmosphere of improved relations.[5] After Beck's Berlin visit, reports came from the German War Ministry concerning a Polish *Putsch* in Danzig. In such an event, what should be the reaction of the First Army Corps in East Prussia? The Foreign Ministry in Berlin replied that it anticipated no surprise from the German or Polish side. The East Prussian Corps was also ordered not to do anything without direct instructions from Berlin.[6]

In spite of public proclamations that German-Polish contacts were very close, in fact, never better, during this time a second picture now came into focus. Increasingly, from 1937, the secret reports of Polish intelligence *Oddział II* gave a pessimistic tone to Polish-German relations. The intelligence communiques observed that, in the last months of 1937, Polish-German relations cooled appreciably and intergovernmental visits were greatly curtailed. The same was observed on the cultural level. The German press described in articles and news items the hard situation and "dark wrongs" which the German minority in Poland had to deal with, in contrast to the few thousand Poles who were living in normal conditions in the Reich and were protected by German law.[7] Polish intelligence observed the end of an era with the liquidation of the League of Nations Commission in Upper Silesia, which was created to supervise the German-Polish railroad network in that highly industrialized region. The German press welcomed this change in Silesia, and called on Poland to live up to the spirit of bilateral agreements, such as the Polish-German Pact of 1934.[8]

From 1937 onward, the Poles perceived intensive border activity. By German law the local border people were to have the proper "political certainty," and the heads of local administration, *Landrate*, would not allow land to be inherited if the heirs did not give a guarantee of political loyalty. This law was primarily directed against the Polish minority living on the eastern borders of the Reich. The area covered by law stretched from East Prussia to Upper Silesia and also covered the Czech border to Bavaria.[9]

During the first part of 1938, Polish intelligence possessed one of the most important secrets of World War II: the key to the breaking of the German military code, which was based on a rotor machine ciphering system patented in 1919, the *Geheimschriftsmachine* called "Enigma."[10] To the Poles, radio-telegraph communication and listening devices were one of the most inexpensive and accurate sources of gathering information on Germany and the Soviet Union. Poland, a financially troubled country, logically turned toward and emphasized this type of work. The use of radio listening intelligence was judged by Warsaw to be more precise than the agent in the field, and Poland was one of the first countries to emphasize the use of this method.[11] Her victory in the Russo-Polish War of 1919-1920 was based in part on the deciphering of Soviet communications. This success left a strong imprint as to the value of this type of intelligence activity. German radio telegrams were read by the Poles from November 1918, observing German rearmament and secret Soviet-German military cooperation, such as joint naval maneuvers in the Baltic.[12]

In 1926 the German navy introduced the "Enigma" machine, followed by the army in July 1928, and the air force in August 1935. The police and other paramilitary units also used the same basic ciphering system.[13] The introduction of this new code forced Polish intelligence to do extensive research as early as 1928-1929.[14] The Polish General Staff organized a group of educators, scientists and professors to help in breaking the "Enigma" code, and to advise the army on important new technical and scientific developments. This Polish "think tank" had members in most Polish universities and polytechnics. The main research center entrusted with the task of breaking the "Enigma" code was located at Poznań University. The director of the Mathematics Institute, Zdzisław Krygowski, organized a series of lectures, which were separate from the university and within closed quarters, to be presented to the most talented twenty students. After three months the most promising students were picked from this group.[15] These selected students were all proficient in the German language. Master's degrees were awarded to this group and they were sent to Warsaw. The most talented were: Jerzy Różycki, Marian Rejewski, and Henryk Zygalski. Their work began in September 1932, in the German Cipher Section named B.S. 4, which had as its main objective the breaking of the German "Enigma"code. The director of this group was Rejewski. This work received the highest level of secrecy. The code name for this work and all radio intelligence activity was *Wicher* (Gale).[16] During this time the German military perfected and modified the machine itself, with a variable number of electrically revolving drums. The cipher and key settings were frequently changed. The *Wehrmacht,* navy, air force, SS and police applied a divergent system of rules in using the "Enigma." Therefore it was necessary to deal with them separately and to work out each innovation. The workings of the machine were complex, based on the system of revolving drums around which 26 letters of the alphabet were placed. The letters of the message were fed by a special typewriter into the "Enigma" machine. The drums of the machine then so disseminated the letters that the Germans considered it almost impossible to break the code without knowledge of the key, which the sender and receiver separately possessed. The drums were changed periodically so that by 1938 there were five separate drums.

Thus, the Polish team tackled what was theoretically considered by the Germans to be unbreakable. These twenty-year-old mathematicians, unversed in the traditional schematic routines of academia, using their linguistic and imaginative abilities, formulated bold new theories of probability, permutations, and group theory. Polish intelligence in turn provided the mathematicians with the latest technology that was available; a small telecommunication factory, AVA, was put at their disposal. This Warsaw-based factory, under the direction of the cryptological section of the Polish General Staff and headed by Major Maksymilian Ciężki, provided the equipment and the technical production. Antoni Palluth, the civilian director, bought a commercial model of the "Enigma" and presented it to the young mathematicians.[17] Polish intelligence also received documents from the French intelligence cryptological section headed by Captain Gustave Bertrand. The French informed the Poles that the Germans were using the "Enigma" system, but that neither they nor the British had broken the German military code.[18] Colonel Mayer, Chief of Polish Counter-intelligence, writes:

Assuming the right premises, that the "Enigma" actually in military use was a derivative from this commercial one, the above-mentioned group of our cryptologists began to work in order to find out what kind of differences and improvements could have been introduced into the military type of "Enigma." Beyond any doubt they should have been located first of all in the inner electric connections of three drums, which constituted the main, essential part of the ciphering mechanism of the machine. Arriving at some clues from the ciphered material of the German navy, our cryptologists to begin with solved the function of the so-called "Umkehrwalze" (reflector). Then they succeeded in reconstructing these inner connections of three drums. Immediately afterward fifteen replicas of reconstructed "Military Enigma" were built in the "AVA" factory under the supervision of Major Cieżki and the technical direction of Mr. Palluth. By the end of 1937 our cryptologists mastered completely the reading of the intercepted German radiograms ciphered by "Enigma." In January 1938, a two-week test was conducted regarding the deciphering of the intercepted "Enigma" material. About 75 per cent of this material was then deciphered. To check this, one day I myself selected radiograms from the intercepted material and ordered them to be deciphered in my presence. The result was perfect.[19]

The key was in the first six letters of the radio telegram. The telegram was coded twice. On the basis of the mathematical theory of cycles, Rejewski's team discovered that the first letters were used as keys in the deciphering of the "Enigma" system. The machines used for this purpose were constructed by the *AVA* factory in 1937. Besides duplicators of the "Enigma," there were cyclometers and complex electronic cryptographic units called *Bomby* (Bombs) with thousands of subassemblies. These cryptographic units were among the first modern computers.[20]

Polish intelligence possessed four listening radio stations located in western Poland. Station No.5 in Starograd covered an area of major interest: the Baltic region, Danzig, East Prussia, and German Pomerania. The Silesian-Czechoslovak Station, No. 3, was located near Cracow in Krzesławice; and in Poznań, Station No. 4, operated for East Germany. The principal central listening center, Station No. 1, was located in a forest in Pyry outside of Warsaw.[21] The value of this information source was at first questioned by the chief of the German intelligence section, Major Jan Leśniak, who expressed his doubts to the chief of the General Staff, Wacław Stachiewicz. It was only after Colonel Mayer informed Major Lesniak of the exact source of the *Wicher* reports that Leśniak received close cooperation from the code bureau chief, Colonel Gwido Langer.[22] From this period onward, detailed information was exchanged regularly between the two Polish intelligence sections.[23]

At this time, East European statesmen and diplomats were reacting to the shift of the balance of power in Europe with a frequent exchange of views. On February 5-8, 1938, Regent Miklos Horthy of Hungary made an official visit to Cracow and Warsaw accompanied by Foreign Minister Kálmán Kánya and his *Chef de Cabinet*, István Csáky. The Hungarians were upset over the projected German moves towards southeastern Europe. Budapest hoped to lay a foundation of cooperation between Poland, Rumania, Yugoslavia, Hungary, and Italy. The other states did not look with pleasure at having Germany as a direct neighbor, but to the Poles this was not a new problem. Warsaw also informed Budapest that a projected Austrian *Anschluss* was very near. The Hungarians held the opposite view. Beck told Kánya that the "Czech case" would be the next problem facing the two nations and that they should prepare a parallel policy to meet the coming events. The Hungarian view was that any territorial changes concerning Czechoslovakia would lead to a conflict, and Budapest was not ready to wage war. The exchange of opinion between the two governments was characterized by a great deal of reserve. Yet an exchange of views was considered positive for future cooperation between the two historically friendly peoples. The dream of Budapest was to dominate, through its noble caste structure, the whole of the mid-Danubian basin, including non-Magyar peoples. To the Hungarians and the Poles, the Czech state presented a barrier, not only to Hungarian plans, but also to Warsaw's dream of creating a common border with Budapest at Prague's expense and to the deflection of German expansion towards the southeast.[24]

In February 1938 Austria was politically isolated, and the German demands increased with each passing day. Chancellor Kurt von Schuschnigg could not rely on any traditional ally or friendly state. Benito Mussolini's Italy was not powerful enough to go it alone to attempt to deflect Germany's moves towards Austria. The Austrian armed forces, numbering under 25,000 were in no position to offer resistance without outside support.[25] Schuschnigg visited Hitler at Berchtesgaden and was faced with demands aiming at the assimilation of Austria into the German economic and political system.[26] The Austrian General Staff had a plan for national mobilization in case of a conflict with Germany. The military plan had been worked out between 1936 and 1937. The code word was *Grenzbeobachtung* (Observe the Border). In six hours mobilization was to take place, first initiated by the border guards, the *Grenzschutz*, made up of five thousand men plus 150 pieces of artillery. The guards were to strengthen the border, destroy bridges and roads, and shield the main mobilization of the Austrian Army. The main defense line was to run from the Alps to where the River Traun meets the Danube. In the interval of eight days, an Austrian army was to be mobilized and concentrated into position, plus a twenty thousand strong reserve force of *Frontmilitz* was to be deployed. Austria based this plan on close cooperation with the Western powers; Vienna counted on assistance directly from Italy via the Brenner Pass, and in time, aid from Czechoslovakia and France from the north and west. The Austrian *Bundesheer* realized that numerically and technically it could not organize a stronger military defense than that of a few days, counting on outside help all along. The Austrian Staff was decidedly ready to stand up to German armed aggression. The army did not have strong National Socialist influence; a clear majority of its troops was dedicated to Austrian independence.[27]

Six weeks after Beck's visit to Berlin, Hitler sent his special representative, Field Marshal Hermann Göring, to Poland on his traditional winter hunting excursion to the Białowieża Forest. On February 23, 1938, Göring told Beck that the reason for the "purges" in the army and diplomatic corps was to give Hitler a free hand to deal with Austria and Czechoslovakia. He also informed the Poles of the Hitler-Schuschnigg conversations. Göring hoped to bring Warsaw closer to German policy by inviting Marshal Edward Śmigły-Rydz to visit German military installations and to meet Hitler. Śmigły-Rydz replied that the invitation should be given at a later date. Marshal Göring devoted the main part of his conversation to the fact that Soviet Russia remained the most serious danger to Polish and German interests, in the face of which the policy of both nations should be "completely harmonized." Göring stated that in Germany, "they perfectly realized that if Poland were defeated in a conflict between Poland and the Soviets, the result would be the swift Bolshevization of Germany." Poland, in Göring's eyes, must quickly become a "bulwark" against Soviet Russia.[28] In a conversation between Göring and Beck, the Polish foreign minister replied that Warsaw's point of view towards Austria had not changed since his visit with Hitler. Poland was interested mainly in the economic aspects of the Austrian crisis: commercial transit through Austrian territory and exportation of Polish coal to that region.[29] Beck's views on closer relations between Berlin and Warsaw were conditioned on a mutually satisfactory solution of the Danzig question and an extension of the Non-Aggression Pact of 1934. The Poles also told Göring that they had interests of a territorial nature concerning Czechoslovakia. Göring assured Beck that the Czechoslovak question would bring Poland no surprises.[30]

The Austrian chancellor found no support from Hungary or Italy, and on March 9, as a last resort to maintain national integrity, he announced a national plebiscite to be held the coming Sunday, March 13.[31] That night Hitler reacted by giving out the order for *Fall Otto*, but the surprise orders found the German army still not ready or completely concentrated on the Austrian border. Hitler gave General Ludwig Beck the order for the preparation and the carrying out of his decision for the army to cross Austria's border no later than the morning of March 12.[32] During this time Polish intelligence worked extensively in Austria. A central intelligence section in Vienna under the code name of *Floryda* sent detailed reports on the German-Austrian crisis. The reports were political as well as military. A special intelligence group was also organized on the border of Austria. Thus in Polish diplomatic circles and from its own intelligence, the *Oddział II* network, Warsaw was well informed of German annexation plans toward Austria.[33]

The intelligence reports stated that up to the last Schuschnigg-Hitler talks of February 12, it was still expected that Austria would be slowly and thoroughly drawn into Germany. The call by Schuschnigg for a plebiscite and his expected victory would hinder, if not stop, the movement towards *Anschluss* and it would also compromise Hitler's personal authority within Germany. Hitler thus would not permit this to happen. It was also observed by the Poles that the Austrian-German union would change the international situation and would strengthen Germany, but that this union would take some time to become complete.[34]

The German General Staff, upon receiving the surprise order from Hitler, had to improvise quickly to put plan *Otto* into a practical military operation. General Theodore von Beck, commander of the 3rd Army *Gruppenkommando* in Dresden, was put in charge of the invasion on March 10. The same day Chief of Staff Ludwig Beck informed General Heinz Guderian that he was to lead eight *Panzer* armored groups as the spearhead of the Austrian invasion. The mobilization covered the following military areas:

III Berlin, IV Dresden, V Stuttgart, VIIBreslau, XI Hanover.

The total German armed forces involved were between 180-200 thousand men.[35] The first use by Germany of mass armed forces in history was augumented by armed civilian police, which were to follow quickly in the wake of the army to quell any civil disturbances during the *Anschluss.* The general Polish intelligence calculation of police units was from sixteen to twenty thousand men.[36] During this time the German police on the Polish and French borders were also mobilized and concentrated.[37] The Austrian-German border was closed and railroad traffic was stopped. On March 10, Polish intelligence noted that all military and police radio stations had stopped their broadcasts; in their place field communication was being used in the mobilized areas on the Austrian border.[38]

Hitler sent a special courier from Berlin to Vienna with a letter demanding that Schuschnigg call off the referendum. At the same time Nazi-inspired distrubances took place in Austria. In order to avoid civil war and a military conflict with Germany, the Austrian chancellor called off the plebiscite on March 11.[39] By this time *Fall Otto* was already in progress with military units converging on Austria. In Bavaria reservists up to the age of 45 were called up, especially technicians and specialists: chauffeurs, pilots, mechanics, engineers, telephone and radio telegraph technicians, etc. In the Munich area all public transportation, such as public buses, railroads, and mail trucks were requisitioned for military service.[40] The events no longer could be defused for Austria. Schuschnigg, under direct pressure from Göring and the Austrian Nazi establishment was forced to resign.[41] On March 12, at 5:30 a.m., the German army crossed the Austrian frontier with no opposition. The Austrian border was closed in six places; the German drive aimed at the cities and Austrian garrison towns of Innsbruck, Bruck, Graz, Linz, Bischofshofen, and Vienna. The use of motorcycle troops and reconnaissance armored vehicles was important in the quick seizure of the terrain, which impressed not only the local population, but even the German army itself. The main role in the taking of Vienna was given to the 2nd *Panzer* Division, which quickly seized the city, without the use of tanks.[42] The Vienna Aspern airport was captured by German aircraft, which took off from air bases near Munich. By 11 a.m., approximately 200 planes had landed and an air force staff with armed guards secured the airport and the radio station. The planes were later used for dropping propaganda leaflets on Austrian towns.[43]

On the afternoon of the 12th Hitler followed his army and crossed the Austrian frontier, symbolically near his birthplace at Braunau. That night he reached Linz, where he met the new Austrian Nazi chancellor, Arthur Seyss-Inquart. On March 13, Seyss-Inquart followed Hitler's orders calling for an annexation which had to take place by a plebiscite of the Austrian people; the 99.08 percent Austrian union vote was a foregone conclusion.[44]

The Austrian army was quickly incorporated within the German armed forces. Some Austrian units in German uniforms were transferred to southern Germany and Berlin in the first days.[45] Before and after Hitler triumphantly entered Vienna on March 13, Austria experienced the rule of the SS and SD. The main public buildings in Vienna were seized, and the Gestapo with SD units arrived clandestinely by air with lists of people from all walks of life and social status to be arrested. The take-over was so quick that it gave the people little chance to leave.[46] The Polish diplomatic mission in Vienna helped many anti-Nazi Austrians and Jews to escape by issuing transit papers and passports. The consulate also used its automobiles to take refugees to the Czech and Hungarian frontiers.[47]

Polish intelligence was given orders to follow closely German preparations directed against Czechoslovakia and to watch the Czech-German frontier.[48] According to Polish estimates, the German-Austrian union opened new political-economic byways into the Danube region for the Reich. Germany now economically controlled more than 50 percent of the total economic trade turnover. Neither Hungary, Yugoslavia, Rumania, Bulgaria, nor Greece was in a position to challenge this economic power. The new German population was more than 73 million in a land area of 83,849 kilometers. Because of the *Anschluss* Germany now had the largest number of neighbors on its borders, and one of the longest strategic boundaries with Czechoslovakia, 206 kilometers.[49] The Austrian addition in the steel, automobile, mining, and railroad industries was great. The seizure and liquidation of the Austrian banks with their gold deposits, and the incorporation of the total Austrian economy into the Nazi Four Year Plan system made Germany, in Polish estimates, the dominant power in southeast Europe.[50]

During the Austrian crisis, the Polish Foreign Minister Beck visited Italy. The purpose of the trip was to get a general orientation of policy from Germany's closest ally. The German government was informed by the Poles that Colonel Beck's visit would not bring about any written understandings between Rome and Warsaw; it was solely for an exchange of views. Beck told Mussolini that Austria had "lost its permanent balance," and it was only a matter of time, "maybe a year, and maybe 48 hours," until Germany would solve the problem. Mussolini was concerned with the prospect of having a German neighbor, yet he agreed that this union was probably unavoidable. Italy was, however, interested in Polish support in the Danube region. Rome hoped to create improved relations between Belgrade, Budapest, and Warsaw as a new bloc to German hegemony. Beck agreed, pointing out that his relations with Hungary and Yugoslavia were developing satisfactorily. The Polish minister pointed out that Poland did not intend to split the Czechoslovak state, but it would not alone "pull the chestnuts out of the fire" for someone else. Mussolini answered that the future of the Czech state did not concern Italy.[51] While Beck was visiting Sorrento, planning to have further discussions with the Italians, the events of the *Anschluss* in which German army units reached the Italian Brenner frontier began to be echoed in Danzig, where that city's senate sent a telegram congratulating Hitler on his Austrian success.[52]

On March 11, news reached Warsaw from its intelligence post in the city of Wilno (Vilnius) that a border incident had taken place on the Lithuanian-Polish frontier at 4:50 a.m., near the village of Trasnikai, Merkine country, Alytus (Olita) district. At that time a Lithuanian border guard (border policeman) had noticed a person in the bushes and ordered him to stop. The stranger answered with a shot; shots were then exchanged by both sides. After a period of time a Polish soldier from *KOP, Korpus Ochrony Pogranicza* (Border Security Guards) was found seriously wounded. A Lithuanian medical assistant and later a doctor dressed the wound, but at 8:40 a.m. the *KOP* soldier died. The next day the body was returned to the Polish authorities. The border incident occurred in the sector of the 23rd *KOP* Battalion. The Lithuanian sector was under the jurisdiction of the Alytus border police guard. The Lithuanian frontier police were under the jurisdiction of the Ministry of the Interior

The Lithuanian General Staff was not directly involved with this incident therefore the army did not order any new security in the region.[53]

The Polish-Lithuanian border had been closed since the Polish seizure of Wilno in 1920, and there had been no diplomatic relations between the two states. The frontier stretched through field and forest and was not fortified, but divided by a trench and border check points. Rail and road traffic were closed. Yet it was fairly easy to cross this green frontier; individual traffic in people and goods was quite extensive, thus incidents were common. Secret unofficial talks between Kaunas and Warsaw had been constantly maintained since the 1920s, but no improvement occurred.[54] Beck was informed that the secret talks were not progressing before he left for Rome. By telephone from Warsaw, the foreign minister was asked to return immediately because of the border incident. From Italy, Beck telephoned Count Szembek with instructions that Poland should avoid any more boundary disputes, and to inform him that he had a plan to settle the problem upon his return. Col. Beck returned through German-Austrian territory by rail. At the border he received the Polish minister to Austria, Jan Gawroński. After hearing Gawroński's reports, Beck gave on-the-scene orders to close the official Polish Ministry office in Vienna and to replace it with a consulate. Talks were also held on the train regarding Central Europe with the Polish minister in Hungary, Leon Orłowski, and Roman Dębicki from Yugoslavia.[55]

In a series of conferences in Warsaw it was finally decided on the night of March 16-17, not to permit the Lithuanians and Poles to settle the problem locally, but to demand through Estonia the establishment of diplomatic relations. Polish troops were put in a state of readiness in the Wilno region. The military commander General Stefan Dab-Biernacki was called to Warsaw. Marshal Śmigły-Rydz quietly arrived by rail to Wilno in Poland, where manifestations of support for the government were held.[56]

The Lithuanian government turned to France, Britain, the Soviet Union, and Germany for support in this crisis.[57] The German minister in Estonia reported that Soviet troop movements had been observed on Russia's western border.[58] Berlin watched the Lithuanian events closely. Its agents, drawn mostly from the German minority in the Baltic states, were well financed and supplied Berlin with extensive intelligence information.[59] Germany feared that at the critical moment of union with Austria, Warsaw might, by ultimatum and military force, bring Lithuania into its sphere of influence, thus endangering East Prussia and the German claims to the Lithuanian Baltic port of Memel (Klaipeda). A military contingency plan, "Case Memel" was drawn up, so that if the Polish army decided to march on Lithuania, German troops from East Prussia would also move into the Memel territory, and naval forces at Swinemunde (Świnoujście) would be sent to the Prussian port of Pillau and to the Memel vicinity. A directive to the German forces was issued by Hitler, in preparation for the military occupation of the Memel region if war broke out between Lithuania and Poland. The plan called for a joint partition of Lithuania, following the course of the Niemen River from the East Prussian frontier eastward to the Dubysa River, then north along the river to a point due east of the northermost projection of the Memel region, then westward to the Baltic coast at the Lithuanian Memel frontier. The Polish government was unaware of the German military contingency plans, and Warsaw did not foresee any military steps against Lithuania, so that no new troop concentration or mobilization was observed by Berlin on the Lithuanian border.[60] The Lithuanian army in March 1938 numbered under 100,000 men and there were no plans for mobilization. On March 19, Kaunas accepted unconditionally the Polish ultimatum of the 18th.[61] From this time onward, the relations between the two states steadily improved, and they drew together in the face of the danger emanating from the west and the east. After the March Ultimatum, Poland stopped all intelligence activity directed against Kaunas. The Lithuanian government let Warsaw know that it would never take any hostile action against Poland. Warsaw considered this a first step in bringing all three Baltic states into its sphere of influence.

CHAPTER TWO

THE CZECHOSLOVAK CRISIS:
THE MUNICH CONFERENCE AND POLISH REACTION

Throughout the Austrian *Anschluss* and the Polish-Lithuanian dispute, Göring informed the Czechoslovak government that entry of German forces into Austria was an internal affair, and in no way would these events hinder the improvement of Czech-German relations.[1] German troops were ordered to keep a distance of 15 kilometers from the Czechoslovak frontier for army formations and 30 kilometers for *Luftwaffe*. Yet constant German flights took place singly and in aircraft formation in the vicinity of Prague and even over the estate of the Czech president in the region of Tabor.[2] The Czechoslovak government protested these aircraft incursions and strengthened the Czechoslovak frontier defense by a police alert on the border.[3] The Austrian-Czech border was fortified by a double defense line. The strongest positions were in the region of Vranov-Znajmo-Mikulov-Breclav. The fortifications were built during the early 1930s and were of medium size. After the *Anschluss* the Czechs strengthened and expanded their fortifications by moving some of their defense lines deeper within their boundaries. The increased cost of this Czech-Austrian sector was estimated at one billion Czech *crowns*. The Czechoslovak government spent over seven billion *crowns* on fortifications up to 1938.[4]

On March 16 the Czechoslovak General Staff observed German troop concentrations in Bavaria and Saxony. Berlin informed Prague that there was "no question of any kind of military preparations." When the German military attaché was invited to visit the Czech General Staff and was given specific information on the German troop movements on the Czechoslovak frontier, he replied that he had heard nothing about this matter, and even if this was the case, it was not directed against the Czech state.[5]

The regular Czechoslovak army in 1938 was made up of approximately 200,000 men; in time of war another 500,000 men could be mobilized, totaling about 13 percent of the population. In peace time the Czechoslovak armed forces were made up of 17 infantry divisions, based on the 1916 French military model, well armed with the latest equipment produced by the Czech armaments industry. Czechoslovak armored and motorized units equalled one-third of all the armor in the German armed forces. Czech artillery was considered to be the most up-to-date in Europe and was sold to other nations, including France.[6] The pre-1938 Czechoslovak border with Germany was heavily fortified along the northern region of Bogumin near the Oder River to protect the Czech northern border from German Silesia. It was in this region that Prague spent over 2.8 billion *crowns* while the area from the city of Liberec to the Elbe River was lightly fortified because of the mountainous terrain and forests in that region, at little more than half the cost of protecting the Silesian border. Because of the natural terrain, the Western Sudeten frontier was lightly fortified with three lines, the last of which surrounded Prague. The purpose of these lines was to slow down the German western drive. The Vltava River region was also fortified.[7] The Slovak region was fortified lightly, with strong forts built only near the city of Bratislava and on the Danube in the area south of Brno. The Slovak-Hungarian border was also fortified, although not to the extent of the Czech-German frontier. The mountainous northern border with Poland was fortified only in the Teschen and Bogumin-Ostrava regions, to the Jabłonków pass and Cadca regions, north of the city of Žilina.[8]

The main German military thrust was foreseen by the Czech Army and its intelligence service. The main attack was to come from the north, between Bohemia and Moravia, across the center of the Czech state to the Austrian frontier, with armor used as the spearhead. It was in this northern area that Czechoslovakia built its strongest fortification, "The Little Maginot Line."[9]

The Czechoslovak government under the direction of President Eduard Beneš and his foreign minister, Kamil Krofta, also feared the rise of pressure from the Western powers. On March 24 Prague perceived that Britain, followed by France, would get involved in the internal minority problems of the Czechoslovak state. Such a British-led *démarche* was considered a handicap, because London traditionally had little interest in or knowledge of Central European affairs.

In a memorandum the British military attaché to Prague, Lieutenant Colonel Stronge reported on the military position of Czechoslovakia after the Austrian *Anschluss*. His main conclusions were as follows:

a. The General Staff consider an attack by Germany on Czechoslovakia within the next year or two probable, as it is impossible to negotiate satisfactorily on the question of the Sudeten Germans. But a declaration by Great Britain to stand by France and Russia would probably prevent it.

b. The General Staff maintain absolutely that the Czechs will fight it out. I think they will if France and possibly Russia come to their assistance at once but not otherwise and perhaps not if the defences are overun before they have properly mobilized.

c. The General Staff know full well that unsupported they must be smashed. It is merely a question as to whether they can offer any form of protracted resistance. I think this is possible in. Slovakia. The Nation is very well organized for war.

d. All plans made on the assumption that France will at least mobilize at the outset.

e. The General Staff consider the most likely strategic objective of Germany will be to cut the country and the Army in two by North and South attacks through Moravia.

f. The frontier defences in themselves possess definite delaying possibilities in the North to large forces and for some time. Sabotage is a great danger. In the South, delay would only be of a very temporary nature, but possibly for a day or two.

g. As regards outside assistance, I am personally doubtful whether France will in fact honour her obligations to the full. As to Russia, my information is that she is unlikely to do so effectively. Yugoslavia will almost certainly remain neutral at the outset.

My reason for expressing a doubt as to France's intentions, which is perhaps outside the scope of this memorandum, is that the assistant French M.A. in Belgrade told me that he felt sure the French peasant could not be induced to fight again for any other object than the defence of his own country and that there was no one in France capable of carrying the people on this issue. He said that the French in their hearts realised this full well . . .

H.C.T. Stronge, Lieutenant-Colonel,
Military Attache.[10]

As German-Czech relations began to worsen Warsaw prepared to react to the German pressure on Prague: Polish-Czech borders were strengthened and notes were sent to Prague on March 22 protesting anti-Polish activity of the Comintern on Czech territory. During this period Warsaw expected pressure from Soviet Russia and France to take a stronger stand on the territorial integrity of the Czech state. Yet in Warsaw's estimate it was concluded that the Czechoslovak governing circles were not prepared to defend that state's independence, and that the Poles were not about to be drawn into a disintegrating political situation, which would run counter to Warsaw's plan of building a new cordon of isolation against Germany without being identified by Berlin as one of the main contributors to Germany's encirclement.[11] The Polish diplomatic personnel observed that France was slowly retreating from Central Europe and that she would concentrate her strength in the west.

Neither France nor Czechoslovakia would cause the war to begin. The Czech state would surrender to Germany and the German Reich would bring the Sudetenland within its territory; the rest of the Czech state would become a vassal of Berlin. Slovakia would not be given over to Hungary by Germany. Italy would be eliminated from southeastern Europe by Berlin. Thus in Europe three blocks were developing: 1) the west, with France and the neutral powers dependent on Great Britain; 2) Germany, dominating Central Europe; and 3) the Soviet Bloc. The formation of these blocs put Poland in a difficult and dangerous situation. Beck, in a conversation with Szembek, concluded that close contact with Rumania had to be maintained and that Budapest must be "stiffened" to the coming Czech crisis. The Muhlstein report from Paris was also discussed.[12]

On March 26 at a dinner given by the Greek minister to Warsaw, views were exchanged between the English Ambassador, Sir William Howard Kennard, and Jan Szembek. The British representative remarked that he did not understand Warsaw's relations towards Prague and that it was quite clear in his view that Germany planned to take over Czechoslovakia and move on to the Ukraine. German expansion to the south into Czechoslovakia would result in Poland being surrounded. The ambassador asked himself why Poland looked on Soviet Russia as such a danger, when Russia was not capable of any sort of military aggression.[13]

Throughout the growing Sudeten crisis a second area of dispute was also developing— the Polish-Czechoslovak border. Czech policy supported nationalistic Ukrainian organizations. A major base after Prague was the Carpatho-Ukrainian city of Uzhgorod (Uzhhorod, Ungvar). The use of this base by the Ukrainian groups antagonized Warsaw because of the effect it had on Poland's large Galician-Ukrainian minority.[14] Czechoslovakia hoped to use the region of the Carpatho-Ukraine, which became a part of easternmost Czechoslovakia in May 1919, as a "bridge" territory to bring about a common border with Russia. The Polish consulate at Uzhgorod watched and reported Ukrainian, Czech, Russian, and German activity in that region.[15] The personnel of this Polish post were, in the majority, members of Polish military intelligence in *mufti*. In contrast, Warsaw supported the Slovak separatist movement and Hungarian irredentism towards Czechoslovakia.[16]

Since 1936, Warsaw and Prague had been gathering intelligence information on each other. The reason for this was that Prague permitted the setting up of a network of Soviet intelligence centers on its territory, and a collaboration was established between Czech and Soviet intelligence.

The Soviets began to use Czechoslovak territory not only against Germany, but also against Poland, using bases in Slovakia and the Carpatho-Ukraine and sending agents across the frontier for subversion and sabotage, especially in the area of Polish Eastern Galicia.[17] Russian military and party intelligence used Czechoslovakian territory to try to make contact through their agents with Polish military figures. The head of Soviet military intelligence was noticed on numerous occasions by Polish counter-intelligence traversing Polish territory to Czechoslovakia with a diplomatic passport. Polish intelligence asked that Czechoslovakia allow the use of its territory as a base for espionage directed against the Soviet Union. This request was refused by Czech intelligence.[18] As a result of this, all intelligence contacts between the two West Slav states were broken until August-September 1938.

During this time Warsaw reinforced the Polish-German frontier to the Czechoslovak border. There were six western Polish border sections: Silesia, Pomerania, Greater Poland, Lesser Poland, and Mazowia. The Polish border had two frontier lines. The first line was regulated by check points and patrols of border roads, railroads, highway transport, and control of individual crossings of the frontier. The border guards also observed people living near the frontier and they set up, with the assistance of the local people, an information network regarding the transit of goods and illegal border crossings.[19] In the area of the second frontier line, which stretched from six to ten kilometers, the main function of the border guards was that of intelligence. These intelligence activities were directed primarily against Germany and the information gathered was sent directly to the central military intelligence centers. The two major centers of this activity were in the cities of Bydgoszcz and Katowice. Bydgoszcz concentrated on Western Pomerania and West Prussia, and Katowice concentrated on German Silesia and Czechoslovakia. These were the two main coordinating centers for gathering information on the Reich, the frontier regions, and also deep within Germany proper.[20] The Bydgoszcz center functioned from 1921. Its most successful action on the frontier was the interception of German railroad traffic crossing the Polish Corridor in closed trains; thus, almost all correspondence by rail between East Prussia and Berlin, and vice versa, was intercepted. This gathered intelligence not only covered military information, but also German intelligence and counter-intelligence reports. This operation was code-named *Wożek* and it functioned from 1934 to 1939. *Wożek* intercepted German mail, noted and photographed the contents and returned it to the "sealed" German mail bags. This was one of the most important sources of information on East Prussia and Germany during the interwar period.[21]

Since 1938 a marked increase in German flights over the Polish borders and the country as a whole was noticed. The Poles did not reciprocate in sending reconnaissance planes over Germany.[22] In January, the Polish-German frontier experienced a marked increase of illegal crossings along the entire length of the border. An estimate made by the Ministry of the Interior and the Polish embassy in Berlin placed the number of people crossing over to Germany yearly at twelve to eighteen thousand. The main reason for these crossings, as admitted by the authorities, was economic, and it was also influenced by the need for workers in German industry.[23] Polish "deep" intelligence "West" had cells in the following German cities: Munich, Düsseldorf, Breslau, and Essen operating from 1933; Piła (Schneidemühl), Leipzig, and Szczecin (two sections) from 1935; Hamburg from 1937; Berlin—two sections, one operating from 1935 and the other from 1938; and Vienna, Königsberg (two sections), and Kwidzyń from 1938. Every section had radio contact with Warsaw.[24] Polish intelligence in the German frontier regions did not use the Polish minority in any espionage work; all agents were organized on a military mode, centrally directed from Warsaw because Poland did not want to give Berlin any cause to persecute the Slavic minority or to bring about an international crisis on the border. Polish workers deep within Germany were recruited to work for Polish intelligence, but they were not recruited from the Silesian or Pomeranian territories bordering Poland.

In contrast, German intelligence used the German minority extensively for espionage against Poland.[25] This network was very active and well organized. Berlin had a very good picture of the Polish military situation on the frontier and also deep within Poland; and it had at its disposal extensive funding, technical apparatus, and a large German minority within Poland. The following elements were also of aid to German intelligence:

1. The Polish-German frontier had no natural barriers. The border was not difficult to cross in either direction, allowing agents easy access.

2. Special communication treaties and understandings between Poland and Germany, i.e., Danzig, made crossing the border a very normal procedure.

3. A general freedom of movement once in Poland was possible.

4. The language problem was not that much of a hinderance because German was in use throughout the country, especially in Western Poland, and many Eastern Germans spoke Polish.

German intelligence had approximately 22 centers of intelligence within Poland, the most important being: Bydgoszcz, Toruń, Grudziadz, Gdynia, Chojnice, and to a lesser extent, Warsaw. Berlin's most important centers directing intelligence activity on Poland were: Danzig, Breslau

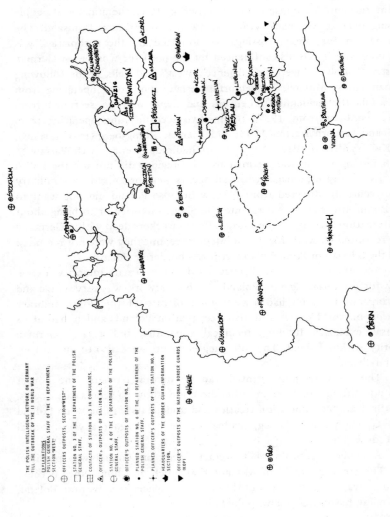

The Polish Intelligence Network on Germany Until the Outbreak of World War II

THE POLISH INTELLIGENCE NETWORK ON GERMANY
TILL THE OUTBREAK OF THE II WORLD WAR

EXPLANATIONS
○ POLISH GENERAL STAFF OF THE II DEPARTMENT;
SECTION "WEST".

⊕ OFFICER'S OUTPOSTS, SECTION "WEST".

□ STATION NO. 3 OF THE II DEPARTMENT OF THE POLISH
GENERAL STAFF.

▦ CONTACTS OF STATION NO. 3 IN CONSULATES.

△ OFFICER'S OUTPOSTS OF STATION NO. 3.

◐ STATION NO. 4 OF THE II DEPARTMENT OF THE POLISH
GENERAL STAFF.

● OFFICER'S OUTPOSTS OF STATION NO. 4.

• PLANNED STATION NO. 6 OF THE II DEPARTMENT OF THE
POLISH GENERAL STAFF.

✦ PLANNED OFFICER'S OUTPOSTS OF THE STATION NO. 6

▶ HEADQUARTERS OF THE BORDER GUARD: INFORMATION
SECTION.

▼ OFFICER'S OUTPOSTS OF THE NATIONAL BORDER GUARDS
(KOP)

(Wrocław, Beuthen (Bytom), Malbork, Königsberg, Stettin (Szczecin), and Berlin.[27] This intelligence activity directed by Berlin increased appreciably during 1938 as shown by the amount of agents observed and caught by Polish counter-intelligence, which augmented three-fold in number. This was considered to be an ominous sign by Warsaw counter-intelligence. Polish intelligence never broke into the German General Staff or into high governmental circles. The same can be said of German intelligence.[28] Since 1936 Berlin had possessed the Polish diplomatic code given to German intelligence by a traitor (a cipher clerk) in one of the Polish embassies in the Middle East. Polish intelligence was aware of the fact that Germany was in possession of this code. The code used by the Ministry of Foreign Affairs was not changed, but new daily tables were added to the code numbers to slow the process of deciphering the messages.[29] The Poles also could easily break the German diplomatic code, but they did not emphasize this type of work because they were short of funds and manpower. Their cryptologists concentrated their major efforts on breaking and reading the "Enigma" military ciphers.[30]

On April 21, 1938, the top secret "Operation Green" was again discussed in Berlin with General Wilhelm Keitel, the successor to General Blomberg. According to the German chancellor the Czechoslovak problem had to be militarily solved, even before the Austrian situation was fully settled. They discussed three political and seven military conclusions:

A. Political

(1) Idea of strategic attack out of the blue without cause or possibility of justification is rejected. Reason: hostile world opinion which might lead to serious situation. Such measures only justified for elimination of last enemy on the Continent.

(2) Action after a period of diplomatic discussions which gradually lead to a crisis and to war.

(3) Lightning action based on an incident (for example the murder of the German minister in the course of an anti-German demonstration).

B. Military

(1) Preparations to be made for political contingencies 2 and 3. Contingency 2 is undesirable because "Green" security measures will have been taken.

(2) The loss of time through transport by rail of the bulk of the

divisions—which is unavoidable and must be reduced to a minimum—must not be allowed to divert from lightning attack at the time of action.

(3) "Partial thrusts" toward breaching the defense line at numerous points and in operationally advantageous directions are to be undertaken at once.

These thrusts are to be prepared down to the smallest detail (knowledge of the routes, the objectives, composition of the columns according to tasks allotted them).

Simultaneous attack by land and air forces.

The *Luftwaffe* is to support the individual columns (for instance, dive bombers; sealing off fortification works at the points of penetration; hindering the movement of reserves; and destruction of signal communication thus isolating the garrisons).

(4) The first four days of military action are, politically speaking, decisive. In the absence of outstanding military successes, a European crisis is certain to arise. *Faits accomplis* must convince foreign powers of the hopelessness of military intervention; call in allies to the scene (sharing the booty!); demoralize "Green."

Hence, bridging the period between first penetration of enemy's lines and throwing into action the advancing troops by the determined ruthless advance of a motorized army (for instance through Pi past Pr).

(5) If possible, separation of the transport movement "Red" from "Green". A simultaneous deployment of "Red" might cause "Red" to adopt undesirable measures. On the other operation "Red" must at all times be ready to come into action.

C. Propaganda

(1) Leaflets for the conduct of the Germans in "Green" territory.

(2) Leaflets with threats to intimidate the "Green."[31]

Three days later in the Czech city of Karlovy Vary, Konrad Henlein, Nazi leader of the Sudeten minority in Czechoslovakia, gave an eight-point list of demands to the Prague government, which he considered to be his "minimum" demands.[32]

During this period the Czechoslovak government had obtained 36 Soviet bombers which were flown to Czechoslovakia. Prague had permission from the Rumanian General Staff to fly over Rumania or to stop in transit. Germany and Poland were very interested to know if Bucharest would also permit the transit of Soviet troops through Rumanian territory. Bucharest let it be known that it would not permit the use of its territory by Soviet forces.[33]

The month of April witnessed a slow turnaround in Prague's policy toward Poland. Dr. Juraj Slávik, the Czech minister in Poland, was instructed to work out a plan for cooperation to facilitate the demilitarization of the Czechoslovak-Polish frontier. The Czechs also were prepared to cooperate with Warsaw against Comintern activity and to stop Communist Polish refugees from organizing on Czechoslovak territory. The Polish Teschen minority would also receive the same concessions as any other minority in the Czechoslovak state. The prerequisite for this improvement of relations was that Beck would drastically alter Warsaw's increasingly cool policy toward Czechoslovakia. Prague promised also to divert its export trade from Hamburg to the Polish port of Gdynia, and a trade and air agreement was proposed. Beck, although displaying a friendly attitude to the Czech proposals, refused to commit himself publicly in support of Prague.[34]

Thus Czechoslovakia relied on an Anglo-French *démarche* in Warsaw. The new French foreign minister, Georges Bonnet, told the Polish ambassador, Juliusz Łukasiewicz, that the French government was in full accord with the British government on the Czechoslovak problem, and if Prague were attacked by Germany, France, as Czechoslovakia's ally, would fight. The British government understood that a possible Franco-German war would become a general European conflict, and Britain would be a direct participant. Thus England would use all its influence to prevent a war between Czechoslovakia and Germany. Bonnet explained to Łukasiewicz that he "left the problem of Czechoslovakia squarely in the laps of Messrs. Chamberlain and Halifax, confirming that I am ready to accept all their decisions and to subscribe to them with my eyes closed." Bonnet stated that as a result of secret Anglo-French talks held in London on April 27 a very negative opinion was formed regarding the indifference and reserve of Warsaw towards German expansion in Central Europe. Paris and London wanted the assistance of Warsaw in their attempt to settle by peaceful means the conflict between Germany and Czechoslovakia, or at least an assurance that the Poles would not take a position in the forthcoming negotiations which could lead Germany to believe that she could rely on Poland. Bonnet stressed repeatedly that "France would always remain true to its alliance with Poland, which is much closer to it than Czechoslovakia,"

and that France and England were only seeking a lasting peace. Łukasiewicz answered him in a friendly and personal manner telling him
what he considered to be of Polish interest:

1. Our formal situation with regard to Czechoslovakia is known:
we are bound only by the Covenant of the League of Nations. In
the realm of mutual relations, Czechoslovakia has done everything
for the past twenty years to poison them.
2. The aim of Polish policy is to maintain the peace, as much so
as the aim of French and British policy.
3. It is advisable to let each country judge what is in its interests,
and to abide by this.
4. Speaking of the interests of Poland, the governments of the
Western Powers often forget that we have two neighbors who can
be equally dangerous.
5. It is small wonder that occasionally there are differences of
opinion between us regarding certain matters in which each of our
countries has a different interest.[35]

In Warsaw both the French and British ambassadors proposed to mediate
the Polish-Czech differences. Beck responded cautiously and enumerated
the old Polish grievances concerning the Polish minority and Communist
activity. The Polish foreign minister received the Czech minister, Slávik,
on May 4 in a friendly manner. During the conversation Slávik declared
that the Polish minority would receive the same concessions as any other
minority in Czechoslovakia.[36] The reason for this move on the part of
Prague was due to pressure exerted on them by Britain and France. The
French ambassador, Leon Noël, told Slávik that to give the Polish minority a more "liberal" treatment than that of the Hungarian or the
Sudeten peoples would bring Poland closer to the policy of the allies,
and that this small Slav minority would in no way threaten the existence
of the Czechoslovak state. Prague feared that a public announcement
of this priviliged minority policy could only cause trouble and bring
about an increase of German pressure.[37]
During the diplomatic *démarche* on Poland to bring that state in step
with the policy of the Western powers, a conference took place in Prague
between the representatives of Britain and France with the Czechoslovak
Foreign Ministry. The Czechs concluded that London had now taken
the Western diplomatic initiative in Eastern Europe. Britain considered
the Sudeten problem to be most dangerous to world peace. The fear
was that an *Anschluss*-style Sudeten crisis would start a war, and that

this must not be permitted to happen. The British General Staff concluded that it would be difficult to aid Czechoslovakia, and that with Austria now a part of Germany, Czech defenses were weakened. It was also pointed out during the conversations that it would be unwise for Prague to count on Soviet aid. The re-emergence and rebuilding of Czechoslovakia would only come about in the future, after the coming victorious war led by the Great Powers, and even then the Czech state should not expect to be rebuilt in the present territorial form. Britain, in the last moment, would enter the conflict, but she would not be drawn in by any diplomatic "game" or "bluff."[38]

On May 20 the Czech state called for partial mobilization because of reported German troops concentrations and Sudeten border incidents. Prague also imposed tight control on telegraph, telephone, and other communications. During this crisis, Beck at first wanted to call off his scheduled trip to Scandinavia, but after a conference in the Foreign Ministry, it was decided that cancelling his flight to Stockholm would be interpreted as a sign that Poland was connected in "some sort of combination with Germany" over the Sudeten question.[39]

By this mobilization Prague was attempting to show a degree of national determination. The reported German troop concentration and border incidents, in addition to other intelligence information, led Czechoslovakia to fear a May "Austrian" style takeover. German units near the frontier were identified from as far away as Bremen and Hamburg. Although May was a normal period for German exercises, the units were judged by Czech intelligence to be substantially beyond normal peacetime levels. The Czechs were also aware that weapons and ammunition were clandestinely transported across the frontier, and that Sudeten German units under the command of the SA and SS were being trained and concentrated in preparation for an uprising and invasion on the eve of May 22, the designated date for the Czech national elections.[40]

At the height of the Czech mobilization crisis, a second exchange of notes took place between France and Poland. Bonnet asked directly for Polish support, because in his view, on "Poland's stand depends the policy of Rumania and partially also that of Yugoslavia." Would Warsaw be willing to make a *démarche* in Berlin concerning the Czech mobilization, similar to the one made by the British government? The second question asked by Bonnet was: "What will Poland do in case German aggression toward Czechoslovakia precipitates an armed conflict with Germany by France and England?"[41] Minister Beck answered on May 24 in the form of instructions to Ambassador Łukasiewicz that Poland was prepared to fulfill her bilateral treaty obligations "within the limits of the present agreements." Warsaw, he added, was also ready to enter into friendly discussions with France "on any new factors based on mutual comprehension of the interests of the two countries." The reaction of Bonnet and Quai d'Orsay was gratefulness for Polish loyalty and assurances to the Franco-Polish entente.[42] The Poles did not want an armed conflict over Czechoslovakia, and Poland would not be the factor that would precipitate such a crisis.[43]

During this period, French foreign policy tried to tie down Polish diplomatic action in a series of direct notes and conversations. Minister Bonnet asked for an official statement regarding Polish military policy from Marshal Śmigły-Rydz through the French ambassador Noël. Quai d'Orsay considered the Polish marshal more pro-French than Minister Beck. However, Warsaw refused to be drawn into any such new declaration because it was suspected that a Polish statement of policy towards Prague might be used by Paris against Poland's interest. At the same time, Warsaw also avoided any commitments to Berlin.[44]

At the end of August 1938, the Czech crisis entered a new stage of development by the active entrance of British diplomacy, represented by Lord Runciman's mission to Prague. The Runciman mediation only strengthened Beck's conviction that Czech policy was no longer free from direct internal interference by Britain and France.[45] On July 27 Poland had asked that if concessions were to be made to the Sudeten German minority, the same should be extended to the Polish and Hungarian minorities. Great Britain was not prepared to recognize Polish and Hungarian claims, which in London's opinion were not "immediate and serious cases."[46] Beck also did not want British or French mediation, as it would have hampered Polish freedom of action. The Polish foreign minister saw the Czech state reacting a step too late for the situation at hand.[47] On September 6, Beneš agreed to most of the demands of the Sudeten German party, but time and the chances for implementation of the German demands within the realm of normal negotiation and in the spirit of goodwill and compromise no longer existed.

On September 12, 1938, Adolf Hitler, in a speech at the end of the Nuremberg Party Congress, gave the "signal" for revolt in the Eger-Asch district of the Sudeten area of Czechoslovakia.[48] The British prime minister, Neville Chamberlain, informed Hitler of his willingness to fly to Germany "to find a peaceful solution to the Czechoslovak crisis."[49] The conference was held at Berchtesgaden on September 15, 1938. It was agreed between Hitler and Chamberlain that the Sudetenland would be detached from Czechoslovakia and annexed to Germany. The German chancellor communicated to the British prime minister that similar demands would be made by Poland and Hungary.[50] Hitler was correct; Foreign Minister Józef Beck officially informed all governments concerned on September 15 and 17, that, if it should come to a plebiscite in the minority regions of Czechoslovakia, Poland would expect due consideration to Polish minorities.[51] The British and French governments requested the Czechoslovak government to reply by September 22 to their communiqué which was marked "secret."[52] The Czech state was to become neutralized; its alliances would be replaced by an international guarantee. Areas with more than 50 percent of German-speaking inhabitants were to be transferred to the Reich.

During this period President Beneš hoped for a Paris cabinet crisis. This cabinet emergency did not materialize; France would not honor her treaty dating back to 1924.[53] Eduard Beneš asked Czechoslovakia's ally, Soviet Russia, for aid in case of war. Russia was, on September 20, willing to give aid "if France remains loyal" and "renders aid." Soviet assistance would also be available if Czechoslovakia would fight alone "as a member of the League of Nations, in accordance with Articles 16 and 17, if, in the event of attack by Germany, Beneš requests the Council of the League to apply the above-mentioned articles."[54]

In Warsaw, Beck faced a delicate situation which historically was not in Poland's interest. A new British, German, French, and Italian "Concert of Europe" was being attempted in September 1938, an organization which had in the past disregarded middle and small nations.[55] The foreign minister saw that Poland could not and should not be the first to start any action against Czechoslovakia, if the Czechoslovak government decided to protect its independence against German aggression. Beck wrote, ". . . should my hypothesis not be correct, Polish policy should change within 24 hours, because in the event of a real European war with Germany we could not be on the side of Germany even indirectly."[56]

During this crisis time Germany suddenly, on September 15, changed the "Enigma" code. This act completely hampered the reading of German military communications, and a "new, long and cumbersome task of solving the internal connections" in the drums was started by the Polish cryptologists, which was not finished until the outbreak of war.[57] Although a new system was introduced in mid-September, the radio network of the SD (Sicherheitsdienst) did not drastically change the code, as did the army and air force. This mistake enabled the Polish team to break and read the SD ciphers, which gave valuable additional German military information to the Polish General Staff.[58] However, the Poles expected this cryptological change in the summer of 1938. Agents of Station No. 3, Bydgoszcz, under the direction of Major Jan Żychoń, reported to Warsaw that in case of an imminent war, the German military intended to put in use two additional drums in the "Enigma" machine. This was considered to be reliable information, coming from an agent in the *Luftwaffe* signal station. This modification of "Enigma" was considered by the Poles as a sign that war was on the horizon.[59]

The Polish ambassador to Berlin, Józef Lipski, was invited by Hitler and Reich Minister of Foreign Affairs Ribbentrop to Berchtesgaden on September 20, for a conversation which lasted more than two hours. Lipski stated that Polish interest concerned only the districts of Teschen-Frystat and access to the railway junction of Bohumin (Oderberg). Poland also supported Hungarian demands for Carpathian Ruthenia, as a "broad barrier against Russia." The chancellor did not commit German policy to support a Polish-Hungarian frontier. With regard to Polish demands for Teschen, he advised the Poles not to move until Germany occupied the Sudetenland.[60]

A formal Polish memorandum was issued to the various interested countries on September 21, 1938:

Memorandum

Polish Embassy

The Polish Ambassador is instructed to inform the German Government that the Polish Government presented a note this afternoon to the British Government, as well as one to the Czechoslovak Government.

The text of the two notes is attached.

Further, the Polish Government has made a written *démarche* in Paris, in which it is demanded that the full consideration necessary should be given to the interests of the Polish population in Czechoslovakia, in like measure as to those of the Sudeten German population.

In this same note to the French Governement, The Polish Government point out that their experiences in the years 1919 to 1921 have left them with no faith at all in Czechoslovak promises or assurances. The Polish Government lay stress, moreover, on their mistrust as regards the efficacy of the steps which have been taken as a result of the conversations carried on in London during the last few days.[61]

In these circumstances, the Czechoslovak government accepted not only the French and British demands, but also a Polish note on

September 21, in which Warsaw asked for the Teschen district and analogous treatment to that of the Sudeten minority.[62] During the Czech-Polish conversations, Kazimierz Papée, Polish minister in Prague, suggested personally to Dr. Krno that Czechoslovakia make a "gesture" by the voluntary cession of the Teschen district and thus "regulate" Czech-Polish relations.[63] The British and French governments reacted by stating that Polish and Hungarian claims would hamper the Sudeten-Czechoslovak settlement. French Foreign Minister Bonnet told Juliusz Łukasiewicz that Polish interests would have to wait until the Czech state received its international guarantee.[64] The French-Polish conversations on September 22, 1938, were reported by Łukasiewicz to the Polish foreign minister. The Polish ambassador told Bonnet that Poland no longer had the same confidence that France and Great Britain would act in Poland's interest. Łukasiewicz stressed that Warsaw has done everything "not to render the situation of France more difficult." He also added that for Poland, "everything in this field depends on France." Bonnet answered that the Polish note was a sign of lack of confidence in France's goodwill. Paris understood the Polish view, but in "order to avoid war it is first necessary to settle the Sudetenland problem," then through international discussions and guarantees of the Czechoslovakian question, Polish interests would also be satisfied. According to the French foreign minister Poland must understand "the gravity of the present situation and must not create the impression" of conducting a policy "similar" to Hitler's.

On the same day, in private conversation, Bonnet and Łukasiewicz again covered the Czech crisis. The ambassador said:

> . . . Polish matters must be treated completely on the same level as the German ones, since they stem from the same principles. . . A solution to the Czech crisis cannot have even the appearance of yielding only to force, or of a cynical division of the territory of Czechoslovakia by others. It must be clear that the idea is to realize the national principles on which the structure of postwar Europe has been based.[65]

Prague also asked France and England to dissuade a Polish *démarche* and sent back no formal reply until September 25. The Polish government knew what a *fait accompli* would mean to British and world opinion, but Polish interest demanded "equality of treatment" going back to May 22, 1938, when Beck informed France that "any concession given by Prague to one minority, and not extended to the Polish would at once provoke tension between Poland and Czechoslovakia."[66]

At this time, the Warsaw authorities intensified the press campaign for Trans-Olza; with few exceptions, the news media supported the demands of the government.[67]

On the day that Chamberlain flew to the second meeting at Godesberg, Sir George Ogilvie-Forbes protested that troops of the "Sudeten-League" crossed the Czechoslovak frontier, and that the town of Asch was occupied by German *Freikorps* soldiers. The British and French governments hoped the German government would avoid such "incidents" and "incursions."[68] Hitler replied by asking Chamberlain on September 22 that the Czechoslovak government evacuate the Sudetenland posthaste as there might be an "explosion. . . which would make all efforts for a peaceful solution fruitless." Germany was prepared to send "troops" and "administrative bodies" to bring about order in the area. The occupation by German authorities was to begin on October 1, 1938. The Czech government was to evacuate between September 26 and 28.[69]

The German demands to the French and British governments were in the form of a memorandum with a map showing the zones and stages of occupation. A second meeting took place and the deadline for acquiescence to German demands was moved to October 1, instead of September 26. Chamberlain left Germany on September 23, still convinced that peaceful means would bring about a solution to the outstanding problems in the Czechoslovak-German dispute.[70]

As tension over the Sudeten problem grew, the Polish government began holding maneuvers on September 22, 1938. Colonel Beck rejected British and French notes of protest against Polish military action.[71] The USSR also reacted on September 23, against ". . .Polish troop concentration on the Czechoslovak frontier," and stated that should Polish forces cross the frontier, Soviet Russia would be compelled to "denounce the Polish-Soviet Pact of Non-Aggression" signed in 1932.[72]

Following the Soviet note, the Polish government denied officially that there were "troop concentrations" on the Czechoslovak border. The Polish army was conducting maneuvers, but in the eastern area of Volhynia. These actions were the "exclusive concern" of the Polish government, which was "not obliged to give an explanation to anyone." Warsaw was aware of 1932 treaty responsibilities and was surprised by the diplomatic *démarche* ofthe USSR.[73]

The exchange of notes between the Soviet Union and Poland, was, in Beck's appraisal, new diplomatic pressure instigated by the Czech president, first through Paris, London, and finally, Moscow. As Foreign Minister Beck subsequently observed:

On two successive conferences at the Royal Castle I submitted a report on the situation and pointed out that according to my hypothesis: (1) the Czechs would not fight, (2) the western powers were neither morally nor materially prepared to intervene in their favour. Russia was also engaged in rather demonstrative action. One could have the impression that they wanted to expose Czechoslovakia and France in their relations with Germany rather than to engage herself. A certain number of Soviet aircraft sent to Czechoslovakia (by Rumania, as we had refused our consent to the transit) introduced a new element increasing the friction between Prague and Berlin, but did not constitute any real assistance to the Czechs. Moscow had already started to mention that she would require transit for her troops over Eastern Little Poland should she have to give real assistance to the Czechs. . . The Czech reply to our note was dated 25 September. It was an answer giving no basis for an amicable solution of the problem. . . It was a striking and quite characteristic feature of the then existing situation that Dr. Benes' letter dated 22 September and announced as very urgent, was only handed over on the 26th. . . It was characteristic because during these three days the famous very arrogant note of the Soviet Government was received, which threatened us with the consequences which would follow any aggressive action by us. . . There was a clear connection between the delivery of Dr. Benes' letter and the date of the Soviet intervention. This detail was also important from the point of view of the attitude we took in connection with this move of the Czech President.[74]

In Prague on September 22, Beneš informed his army staff that he would approach Poland to obtain her neutrality, for the price of the loss of the Teschen territory.[75] Dr. Kamil Krofta, the Czechoslovak foreign secretary, informed Warsaw of Prague's agreement in principle on the opening negotiations concerning Teschen.[76] A letter dated September 22 was also sent by special plane to President Mościcki from Dr. Beneš on September 26, 1938. The Czechoslovak president wrote:

At a moment when the destiny of Europe is at stake and when our two nations have a genuine interest to lay solid foundations of a confident collaboration between the two countries, I address to Your Excellency a proposal to re-establish friendly relations and a new collaboration betwen Poland and Czechoslovakia.
I therefore suggest to Your Excellency, on behalf of the Czechoslovak State, a frank and friendly settlement of our differences concerning the problems of the Polish population of Czechoslovakia.

I should like to settle this question on the basis of accepting the principle of frontier rectification. An understanding concerning our mutual relations would naturally be the logical and immediate consequence of such an arrangement. If we reach an agreement— and I am confident that this will be possible— I will regard it as the beginning of a new era in the relations between our two countries.

I should like to add, as former Foreign Secretary and present President of the Republic, that Czechoslovkia does not have, at the present moment, any obligations or treaties, secret or public— nor did she ever have any— which would by their meaning, aims or intentions damage the interests of Poland.

With the consent of the responsible ministers, I present this suggestion to Your Excellency confidentially, but also personally, so as to give it the character of a firm undertaking. I should like to make this a matter to be settled between our two nations alone.

Aware of the delicate character of our mutual relations and realizing how difficult it has always been to improve them in normal times by ordinary diplomatic and political means, I am endeavouring to use the present crisis for breaking down the obstacles of many years and for creating at one stroke a new atmosphere. I am doing so in full sincerity. I am convinced that the future of our two nations and their future mutual collaboration can only be definitely assured in this manner.

Believe me, etc. . . . [77]

President Mościcki accepted both notes, and with a note and a personal letter answered the Czech head of state on September 27, stressing the "urgency" and the need for a "courageous" stand on the part of the Czechs. He also wrote that agreement was possible if there was an immediate cession of lands about which there was no question as to its Polish character. Also a mutual agreement could be reached between Poland and Czechoslovakia as to the details for a plebiscite in territories with a large percentage of Poles.[78]

The Polish envoy, Kazimierz Papée, urged the Czech foreign minister that ". . . a solution of the Polish-Czechoslovak dispute should be reached outside the scope of the Munich conference," in the "shortest time" feasible.[79] The British government was informed by its Warsaw ambassador, Kennard, of the Polish-Czechoslovak exchange of notes and letters, and asked Prague "to abandon diplomatic maneuvering" and start negotiations on the cession of Teschen and Frystat to the Poles.[80]

Beneš hoped that both France and Poland would stand by Czechoslovakia in rejecting the Godesberg Memorandum. It was expected by

Prague that Poland would be neutral even in the last resort; the price would be territorial cession of certain districts in Czechoslovakian Teschen. Prague and Warsaw were the conerstones of French East European policy. In the tense atmosphere of East Central Europe, it was inconceivable for Dr. Beneš to believe that the post-Versailles system was no longer operative for France.[81]

The Czechs refused the Godesberg Memorandum forwarded by London on September 24, 1938. That evening at 10:30 mobilization was called by the Prague government; rail and telephone communication was cut off between Germany, Poland, and Hungary.[82] France, as Czechoslovakia's ally, also ordered mobilization of her army.[83]

British diplomatic circles again made German contact stating that if Berlin was prepared to give way "on the form," the British government "would be prepared to push through all demands with the Czechs and French."[84] Prime Minister Chamberlain wrote to Hitler:

> I am ready to come to Berlin at once to discuss arrangements for transfer with you and representatives of the Czechoslovak Government together with representatives of France and Italy, if you desire. I feel convinced we could reach agreement in a week.[85]

Anglo-French talks were held in London on September 24. Chamberlain's aim was to dissuade France from mobilizing. The British government informed Paris that a personal delegate sent by Prime Minister Chamberlain would fly to visit Hitler with a message from Chamberlain. Quai d'Orsay agreed to the trip of Horace Wilson. Hitler saw Wilson and stated:

> Whether by negotiation or whether by the exercise of force, the territory would be free on the 1st of October; and if he did not know for certain that the Czechs accepted in the course of the next two or three days the territory might well be cleared of Czechs before the 1st of October. On reflection he must have an affirmative reply within two days, that was to say by Wednesday.[86]

In this tense international atmosphere during the Hitler-Wilson conversations, Poland and Czechoslovakia again exchanged notes on September 26 and 27. The Polish government demanded: (A) the immediate cession of lands about which there was no question; and (B) mutual agreement on details for a plebiscite in the territories with preponderant percentages of Poles.[87]

Another action undertaken by Polish diplomacy was to inform the German Foreign Office as to what were Warsaw's immediate and important interests, in answer to Minister Ribbentrop's constant inquiries as to Warsaw's plans toward Czechoslovakia.[88] Józef Lipski reiterated to the *Auswaertiges Amt* the Polish stand on Teschen. Hitler knew about the Polish specific claims towards Teschen-Frystat and the Bohumin (Oderberg) railway junction. The Polish ambassador stated that Warsaw's demands were understood by the German chancellor when they were first presented, at his request, on September 20, 1938.[89] Beck's apprehensions that Berlin might disregard Polish interests were based on his observation of the new German *Realpolitik*. He feared that German military occupation in "rough-and-tumble" way of Czechoslovakia, would clash with Polish interests in Bohumin and Teschen.[90] The Poles hoped that no direct military conflict would occur over the Bohumin region. But fear of a crisis did not deter Beck from officially informing Germany that Warsaw "would not retreat" from its position on Western Teschen and Frystat, and would "resort to force" if its interests were not recognized. It was agreed: Bohumin would be part of the boundary of Poland. Western Frydek and Moravska Ostrava were to hold a plebiscite between Germany and Poland.[91]

Hitler agreed to hold a conference with Italy, France and Great Britain at Munich on September 29-30. The Czechoslovak government was not present; Poland was not invited. The Teschen problem was not solved. There was no far-reaching boundary settlement in the Carpatho-Ukraine. It was agreed at Munich that if Polish and Hungarian claims were not met in three months, another Four Power Conference would convene.[92]

On September 29, 1938, Poland reacted to the Hitler-Chamberlain meeting by asking Prague for a favorable answer in the shortest time to its third *démarche*. Warsaw stated that a solution of the Polish-Czechoslovak dispute should be reached outside the scope of the Munich decisions. Papée, the Polish representative, proposed that Czechoslovakia give Poland a "favourable answer" to the Warsaw note of September 27.[93] Colonel Beck, writing on the Munich Conference, stated:

Thus we had to face two events:
(1) An extension of the German territory next to our very frontier and in the vicinity of Cieszyn Silesia, particulary valuable for us.
(2) The fact that European territories were divided by a conference not based on law or international order, by a mere congress of the representatives of Four Powers, which did not take into account the opinion and the interests of other countries. This method of action not only destroyed the very foundation of the League

of Nations Covenant, which should be binding for two powers
taking part in Munich, but also disregarded the most elementary
principles of respect for state sovereignty and the inviolability of
its territory.[94]

The Czechoslovak government did not answer the Polish appeal. Prague
replied to Warsaw only after the Munich Conference was over, and Dr.
Beneš agreed to its decisions. The Czechoslovak response on September
30 was for Beck, "completely inadequate and dilatory."[95] Prague
stated in its note that it

. . . wished to avoid the giving the Czech nation the impression
that advantage was being taken of the difficulties which at present
confronted Czechoslovakia. By its procedure the Czech government wished to make it plain that this was a matter of an act of
good-will resulting from its own initiative and its own free choice.
This was considered important with regard to future relations . . . [96]

On Polish specific demands for territorial cession and a plebiscite,
Prague took a negative stand, using the argument that in negotiations
concerning the German minority it had to refuse to hold a plebiscite
and to make territorial cession until the frontiers had been definitely
marked. On September 30, the Prague government issued the following
seven-point program:

(1) The Czechoslovak government would give the Polish government
its solemn assurance that delimitation of frontiers and the consequent
territorial cession would be realized under whatever conditions might
prevail, regardless of the international situation. The Czechoslovak
Republic was willing in this regard to make such a declaration to France
and Great Britain as well, and to accept these countries as guarantors
of the Polish-Czech Treaty.

(2) Division of territories would be accomplished on the basis of a
partition of the districts under dispute, according to a population census.

(3) A Polish-Czech Commission would be appointed not later than
October 5, 1938, the purpose of which would be to regulate matters
of options and economics.

(4) This Commission would finish its work by October 31.

(5) The date of the territorial cession would be set.

(6) A joint communiqué would be issued on the reaching of an
agreement for frontier rectification.

(7) The territorial cession would be executed, at the latest, by December
1, 1938.[97]

The Polish Telegraph Agency, PAT, issued an official communique on the evening of September 30, which stated: ". . . the (Czech) note in an astonishing manner, wholly unexpected in the face of today's serious situation, limits itself, unfortunately, to truisms, by means of which the Czech government evidently essays to prolong the situation and to avoid executing its previously made declarations."[98] The communique lamented the fact that Prague had superficially treated "Poland's clear and categorically put demands." This unexpected reply of the Czech government was the reason why the Polish government replied without delay in a clear and precise manner, demanding satisfaction of Poland's just and motivated claims. The responsibility for failure to settle this matter would rest on the Czech government.[99]

Beck's reason for haste was that the claims between Warsaw and Berlin conflicted in the area of Northern Teschen. Polish *desiderata* were a known fact; Lipski informed the German government of Polish specific claims towards the Bohumin Junction on September 20. The Godesberg map was not shown by the German Foreign Office to the Polish government. Only through British and French channels was the map revealed to Warsaw. It was clear that the Germans planned a *fait accompli* in the Bohumin area. On September 28 German and Polish maps were studied by Lipski and Weizsäcker. The German claims did conflict with the Polish. Ambassador Lipski stated that the matter must be settled the same day.[100] Thus, Germany finally agreed that the Bohumin region would be within the national boundary of Poland. Colonel Beck responded to the Polish-German dispute by calling a conference on September 30 at Warsaw Castle; those present were Marshal Śmigły-Rydz, President Mościcki, Beck, Sławoj Składowski, and E. Kwiatkowski. It was agreed that an ultimatum was to be delivered to Prague before 12 p.m. on September 30. The Polish note called attention to the "impossible" state of affairs in Teschen Silesia, further recalling President Eduard Beneš' acquiescence in principle to cession of territory about which there was no question as to its nationality make-up, and a plebiscite to be held in territories inhabited by a mixed population. The Polish government demanded the cession, without delay, of two districts, Teschen and Frystat, and an official Czech answer was expected by October 1, 1938.[101] The note further read that representatives of the governments of France and Great Britain had informed the Polish government that the Czechoslovak government had agreed to Polish demands in their entirety. This information had not been confirmed, and the promises had not been kept.[102]

The Warsaw note stressed that "the Polish Government no longer has any confidence in declarations made in the name of the Czechoslovak Republic." and therefore categorically demanded: (A) immediate evacuation by the Czech army and police of territories indicated on the map and the transfer of these territories indicated into the hands of Polish military officials; (B) evacuation of the above territories within twenty-four hours; (C) cession of the remainder of Teschen and Frystat districts within ten days.[103] Poland's ultimatum was not coordinated with Germany; Warsaw asked only of Berlin for its "benevolent neutrality" in case of a Polish-Czech conflict.[104]

Great Britain again offered mediation in the Polish-Czech dispute through Ambassador Kennard in Warsaw, on behalf of Chamberlain. On his part, the British ambassador added that if Poland rejected or had any objection to mediation by the prime minister because of his participation in the Munich Conference, then Great Britain would be willing to accept any other intermediate agent, for example, President Franklin D. Roosevelt of the United States. At the same time, British and French ambassadors in Berlin appealed to the Reich government to restrain the Poles from taking military action against Czechoslovakia.[105]

The British view was that Poland was taking the consequences of the ultimatum into her own hands by not recognizing that the Munich Pact provided for a peaceful settlement of Polish claims for Teschen and Frystat. French Ambassador Noël also communicated to the Polish Foreign Office that Paris supported the British initiative. Both nations received a negative reply from Warsaw.[106] An appeal to Poland was also made by President Roosevelt, delivered by the United States ambassador, A.J.Drexel-Biddle, in which Roosevelt expressed the conviction that Poland would avoid open conflict, and through peaceful negotiation settle the difficulties between her and Czechoslovakia.[107]

The Polish ultimatum was accepted by a Czech note.[108] In the note the Prague government recalled that the Munich Pact called for a three-month period for Polish-Czechoslovak negotiations. In view of the Polish note of September 30, and "forced by the circumstances," the Czech government accepted the Polish conditions and suggested a meeting of Polish and Czechoslovak experts to discuss details of territorial cession. Prague also asked that rail communication on the Bohumin-Žilina line not be interrupted.[109]

The geopolitical changes stemming from the Munich Agreement constituted a major defeat for Polish foreign policy. Warsaw was not invited or consulted upon the outcome of the Four Power decisions which directly concerned Polish policy and national interests. Beck reacted independently without prior consultation with Germany, demanding by ultimatum from Prague the Teschen territory. Czechoslovakia was forced by the chains of events to accept the Polish terms.[110]

In their intelligence reports the Poles observed the total breakdown of political and territorial stability in East Central Europe. Prague was not prepared to resist German aggression by itself, relying instead on the support of the Anglo-French powers to intervene with Hitler on its behalf. Polish intelligence judged that the Czechoslovak army was not prepared to fight, even if there was a will to resist, because Dr. Beneš' government would not order or permit the start of any hostilities. The Sudeten-Czech crisis in the intelligence reports was closely connected with the March Austrian *Anschluss*. The key role in these two events was the leadership and judgment of Adolf Hitler. In February 1939 Polish intelligence reported that the main elements forming Hitler's views of the international situation were as follows: (A) the unpreparedness of the Western Powers and their readiness to keep the peace in Central Europe; (B) the weakness of Soviet Russia; and (C) the support of the Axis Powers, especially Italy, for German expansion.[111]

Thus German diplomacy used the Sudeten minority question by presenting through the Henlein movement the maximum demands in the shortest period of time, giving Czechoslovakia very little time to consider or even to counter these demands. There were three basic phases of German action directed against Czechoslovakia: 1) Germany presented a series of radical demands on Sudeten autonomy within the Czech state. Prague still hoped to receive support and aid from the Western Powers and Soviet Russia. 2) Hitler was aware that Great Britain was ready to compromise by diplomatic means, by sending the Runciman Mission to Czechoslovkaia. At Nuremburg, Hitler publicly told the world that Germany had a direct interest in the Sudeten minority, thus bringing about internal Czechoslovak disruptions. A conference at Berchtesgaden (Godesberg) took place between Chamberlain and Hitler over the Sudeten question, without any positive results. 3) Hitler gave Chamberlain an ultimatum demanding Czech territory and the total reorganization of Czechoslovakia. At Munich Chamberlain persuaded Hitler to revoke the ultimatum; at the same time, Germany demanded and received more Czech territory than Hitler asked for at the first Berchtesgaden meeting.[112]

Hitler's victory at Munich brought Czechoslovakia under direct German influence. Berlin controlled not only the Czech Sudeten territory, but also new sources of raw material, industry, and manpower that had been militarily trained. In the Polish estimate, Germany emerged as the leading power in Europe becaue of the Munich Conference.

The German mobilization directed against Czechoslovakia was organized in secret and on the Austrian model; in both cases Germany was prepared to use military force. The German army camouflaged its mobilization activities. This led Polish field observers to make inaccurate reports.[113]

In September 1938, Germany mobilized approximately fifty divisions, divided into five groups: Generals Block and Rundstedt from Silesia commanded the north; Generals Leeb and List the south, from Austrian territory; and the center from Germany proper was headed by General Reichenau. The German concentration directed against Czechoslovakia involved approximately 60 to 70 percent of the German armed forces. On the Polish-German border in East Prussia the German divisions remained in place except in Silesia, Pomerania, and Brandenburg.[114] The official reason for mobilization was a call for a general national levy of over a half million men to build fortifications in the west. There was a lack of trained officers and the military equipment of the reserve units was not up to modern standards. The air force had at its disposition approximately 3500 airplanes directed against Czechoslovakia and 1500 against France.[115] The important role of the German *Luftwaffe* was to destroy the Czechoslovak system of fortifications by bombing. It was estimated by the Poles that the light concentration of forces on the Czech frontier foretold that high German government circles expected the Sudeten crisis to end quickly.[116]

* * * * * * * * * *

During this time, on September 23, 1938, a Polish army group began to be formed; its purpose and plan was the occupation of Teschen and Frystat.[117] The military preparations were made in haste.[118] General Władysław Bortnowski was designated by Marshal Śmigły-Rydz to lead the operation. The army group was called *Samodzielna Grupa Operacyjna Śląsk* (Independent Operational Group Silesia.[119] Śmigły-Rydz's instructions were to be ready by October 1 to fight, or to occupy Teschen, no matter how negotiations turned out between Warsaw and Prague. According to Smigly-Rydz, the question of Teschen had to be settled. In case of a direct conflict or war, Bortnowski's operational group would not get any aid until after a period of seven days. Bortnowski's army group strength consisted of three infantry divisions with none up to full complement (21st division, 23rd division, and 4th Pomeranian Poznań

Division) including artillery, a brigade of cavalry, a brigade of armor, and a Trans-Olza Corps. The Army Staff Headquarters was set up in the town of Skoczów. The plan of military action envisioned a direct attack by the 23rd division under Colonel Sadowski on the line of Czech fortifications running from the area of Trzyniec to Frystat; the 21st and 4th divisions commanded by Colonel Kustronia and Brigadier General Abraham would attack across the mountains in the south, below the forces of the 23rd division, and surround the Czech forces.[120]

At the same time, Polish-Czech army contacts remained active, and open information was exchanged between Czechoslovak General Hrabczyk and General Bortnowski as to the means of implementing the Polish occupation. A ten-day period of military occupation was planned in Prague to which Warsaw agreed. General Bortnowski and his newly organized staff were not familiar with and originally took no interest in the Teschen area. The territory was for the most part "new" to them.[121]

On September 28, the personnel of the "Independent Operational Group Silesia" were found to be lacking and inadequate. The Polish army staff *Śląsk* needed five officers, one language translator and a code officer, none of which were furnished by the Warsaw General Staff.[122] The Army Command also needed supplies and personnel. Artillery Command was made up of four officers. This was insufficient: a deficiency of one officer and lack of trained personnel still persisted. Also, there was a need for one clerk and a draftsman. Air Force Command was composed of nine officers and this number was sufficient. Anti-Aircraft Command Staff did not show up with full strength; the command had two officers, but four were needed. Positions were filled temporarily by officers from other commands. The Communication Command was made up of three officers, which was inadequate; one additional officer was needed as well as other qualified personnel. The commander for the armor brigade was not present, nor was there any one who could instruct the general personnel in the use of tanks and armor. There was also a lack of weapons. The whole formation of the different Polish army staffs lacked planning and organization. The Medical Crops was organized properly to meet the needs of the *Śląsk* army. Bortnowski's infantry was composed of 29 battalions; only three were properly trained and battle ready.[123] Ordnance and artillery also were not up to full strength. The artillery sections available were the following:

29 sections	75mm,
49 sections	100mm,
4 sections	105mm,
6 sections	120mm,
8 sections	155mm,
6 sections	220mm,

Total: 102 sections

Air power at the disposition of *S.G.O. Śląsk* consisted of five squadrons of fighters, two squadrons of light bombers, and one reconnaissance squadron. The total air support was 103 airplanes, including ground and anti-aircraft companies.[124]

Army Intelligence Section *Oddział II* was not prepared to cope with the Czech action of sealing the border which took place on September 23. Radio communication with western Teschen and Frystat was weak due to the Czechoslovak authorities finding and liquidating a number of Polish radio stations. It was virtually impossible for the Polish military to get even a general picture of Czechoslovak strength or activity.[125]

During the time of military build-up and organization of the "Operational Army Group Silesia," there were many "suspect" people who freely traversed the area of military concentration without hinderance or any type of control. Polish army *Śląsk* counter-intelligence was at this time being formed by improvisation. The officer for this section came from Warsaw without any system for operating or developing counter-espionage. He came only with orders; he was not supplied with any means of transportation or with money.

In the face of mounting military pressure and the organization of a formal plan for military action, army intelligence was found lacking in knowledge of Czech armaments, such as certain types of airplanes, tanks, uniforms, etc. This information was not sent until later to the Polish Teschen army by Warsaw; thus all these data were gathered by the *Śląsk* army presently. There was also a need for Czech administration maps, railroad maps, telephone communication maps, drafts of areas of public concentration, and plans showing public buildings and military objects. Several language translators were needed, as no officer in *Oddział II* knew the Czech or Slovak language.[126]

On September 24, 1938, army staff espionage had at its disposal the following Teschen individuals: an officer in the Czech Army Reserve in charge of the National Guard in the city of Trzyniec, and an agent in the directorate for the building of Czech fortifications in the Teschen area. The total number of agents was 14, under the direction of a Captain Piasecki.[127]

Piasecki encountered many problems in carrying out his work. He needed a qualified and competent assistant because the job of taking care of 14 agents was a difficult one. Piasecki required close liaison by radio, etc., to keep his chain of agents active. The mobilization of the Czechoslovak forces on September 23 found the espionage organization in an unsettled state due to the fact that there was a shortage of qualified personnel, but this problem was alleviated by recruiting women agents.[128] In charge of defensive espionage was Captain J. Karszniewicz. His job was to censor and control the terrain on which the Polish army Śląsk would operate. Following incipient organizational difficulties, harmony was reached by both staffs, intelligence, and counter-intelligence. During this period, Polish intelligence concentrated also on intercepting Czech radio communications. The work of radio interception did not bring about any new information, because it was difficult for untrained personnel to differentiate the Czech radio military codes from German, Hungarian, or amateur wave lengths.[129]

On the basis of S.G.O. Śląsk army information at hand, and after a period of a few days, Bortnowski's forces were generally prepared for military action. There was, however, no general organization that would control the different "independent" espionage groups which were free of military supervision.[130]

Poland's ultimatum of September 30, demanding Teschen, Frystat, and Bohumin from Prague forced the Czechoslovak government to yield the next day. General Bortnowski was ordered to march into Teschen.[131] On October 2 Czech army automobiles carrying white flags arrived with General Hrabczyk and other Czech officers wearing white armbands. Both parties proceeded to exchange last-minute information with the Polish representative General Malinowski, on the Teschen bridge which cuts the city in two.[132] It was a "business-like," prearranged formality. General Bortnowski appeared also on the Teschen bridge, and a moment later, the first Polish patrols marched across, followed by cyclists, the mountain troops (Podhalańskie) and a National Guard battalion.[133] The population of the city of Teschen welcomed Bortnowski's army.[134] On October 4 at twelve o'clock, the Polish forces occupied the towns of

Trzyniec and Jabłonków, and two divisions, the 21st and the Poznań-Pomeranian, made contact with each other.[135] As the military occupation proceeded, it was discovered that the civilian administration was not ready to take over the responsibility of government from the military. The problem of coping with an emergency situation, such as police, post, railroads, schools, industry, etc., forced the military to take over most of the normal functions of civil administration.[136]

The total amount of troops and equipment of Independent Operational Group Silesia, combative state, on October 1, 1938, was the following:[137]

officers	1,522
non-commissioned officers	6,208
troops	28,236
horses	8,371
wagons	2,496
field kitchens	250
radio stations	176
automobiles	267
trucks	707
motorcycles	459
tanks	112
airplanes	103

In the chaotic situation the Polish military government issued new public laws. On October 3 the restrictions on the sale of alcohol were announced, and a notice was given that arms and munitions without permit, in private hands, were to be turned over to the police before October 5, 1938.[138] The Communist party was declared illegal in Teschen on October 20.[139] All schools and public places began to use the Polish language by order of the Silesian district delegate, Leon Malhomme.[140] Bortnowski's army moved into position to occupy the area of Bohumin Junction and the Karvina industrial complex. The Karvina area was occupied by Polish light tanks and cyclists on October 10.[141] At this time, Polish intelligence *Oddział II* reports notified General Bortnowski's staff that German *Ordnung* or civilian armed guards had opened fire on Czechoslovak border guards in the city of Bohumin.[142] It was feared that German *Ordnung* forces might seize the area before the Polish army began its occupation.[143] Bortnowski contacted Czechoslovak General Hrabczyk and asked him if it was possible to take the Bohumin area ahead of schedule; Hrabczyk would not agree to this change of plan. He stated that he did not have the authorization to change the agreed upon time-table for Polish occupation, and that both Warsaw and Prague would have to be consulted.

General Wacław Stachiewicz, chief of the Polish General Staff, advised General Bortnowski by telephone that there was no need for independent action outside of the prearranged plan of occupation. But Bortnowski was not convinced by the assurance of the Warsaw General Staff. He set down a plan for the occupation of Bohumin three days earlier than scheduled. A conversation took place between Generals Hrabczyk and Bortnowski. The Polish general argued that Bohumin was a large, complicated railroad station, and that it was necessary to send Polish railroad personnel to acquaint themselves with the technical equipment of the junction. General Hrabczyk agreed to this purpose. A six-man railroad team, under the command of a Lieutenant Mazur, was sent to Bohumin to take and hold the railroad station. To the north, a mile from Bohumin, Bortnowski gave orders to build a bridge across the Olza River, in case it should be necessary to seize that city. A military force of forty men was also sent to the German border to guard against the infiltration of armed elements, under the command of Lieutenant Colonel Zycha. Two cavalry squadrons, under Colonel Dworak, were four miles outside of Bohumin. In addition, two companies of regular police were put on alert.[144]

The night of October 8 General Bortnowski was informed by telephone that Czechoslovak troops were evacuating Bohumin two days ahead of schedule. The Polish General telephoned General Hrabczyk stating, "Bohumin is in a mess, your company has left the scene, please straighten this out." General Hrabczyk appeared in Bohumin and the Czech army returned. During this period, Polish troops also moved in and remained along with Czechoslovak military to prevent any type of clash or incursion by the German armed forces. The formal Polish occupation of Bohumin took place on October 10 and 11.[145] General Bortnowski became the military governor of Teschen until December 10, 1938.[146]

During this period, *Samodzielna Grupa Operacyjna Śląsk* received orders from Marshal Rydz-Śmigły to occupy the southeastern area of Czech-Polish delimitation in the region of Cadca (Czaca). Polish military action began on November 25, 1938, at 9 A.M. General Bortnowski gave command of the operation to Colonel Nikolas Bołtucia, commander of 4th Infantry Division and its staff. An armor squadron also joined Bołtucia's group. All military elements were notified by telephone.[147]

The Czechoslovak army was in fortified positions situated in mountainous terrain, protecting the railroad line leading to the city of Cadca and to western Slovakia. The Czechoslovak army resisted the Polish encroachments.

Military action began in the region of Kiczera and the Jaworzyna area, north of Cadca. One Polish officer and eleven soldiers were wounded: of this number two died.[148]

At twelve o'clock the Prague authorities asked for a truce; the Poles, after consulting Warsaw, agreed. But from the military technical point of view, military action continued until 1300 hours on November 25, 1938. Around 1600 hours the Czechoslovak army started military action which was answered by the Polish forces. The Czechoslovak forces retreated from their positions at 1700 hours, and a complete break in the engagement ensued. The Czechoslovak-Polish Truce and Boundary Commission agreed on November 26, 1938 to the southern boundary of Teschen in the region of Cadca.[149]

In the region of Jabłonków in the Carpathian Mountains, Polish troops in battalion strength engaged Czech forces.[150] Due to the mountainous terrain military action was very difficult. The Polish army Śląsk forgot to use mortars, the most effective type of artillery for use in rugged terrain.[151] Army supplies were completely inadequate due to the use of horse and wagon transport, an ineffective method in the local geography which hampered movement. The Polish infantry reacted well under fire, although certain groups and individuals became dangerously over-curious. At the sight of wounded comrades many soldiers became eager for forward action. But the general inclination of the Polish troops was to treat the military expedition with levity. Discipline in some sections was weak; with the appearance of Czech airplanes the brigade started to shoot at the planes without result. The Czechoslovak planes dropped their bombs an open fields without doing any damage to the Polish forces. The Czech infantry reacted nervously during military action with wild fire. Czechoslovak field artillery on the whole was accurate and well-guided. Polish radio listening devices reported that Czech artillery commands were given in the German language.[152] The placement of Czech machine guns and the use of terrain was well thought out. Movement of Polish troops was signaled by the Czechoslovaks with rocket flares. Notice was given by the Czechoslovak army that if the Poles would continue to advance, they would be further resisted. Among the captured Czech soldiers there were five Slovaks. They asked to be set free because they were "brothers of the Poles" and had no reason to fight. The Slovaks were released by the Polish officer in charge.[153]

Polish military communication by radio and telegraph was difficult. The lines were overtaxed in every army group by unnecessary conversations. Cooperation between the different units raised problems. There was another difficulty: the military reports reaching the Staff Command Base were not completely accurate, nor did they confirm the military situation. Seven Czechoslovak prisoners were taken. Losses to the Polish forces amounted to two dead and ten wounded. The Czech losses were four killed and fourteen wounded.[154]

The population of western Slovakia was generally hostile in the new military occupied territories. Incidents did occur when civilians fired on Polish troops, in even what were thought to be friendly areas. There were incidents in the Filkowa region and Kulisko, southwest of the town of Mosty.[155]

Meanwhile, Czechoslovak-Polish negotiations reached a general agreement in which Polish claims of 1918 to the city of Cadca and thirteen mountain villages were amended. Poland occupied only the Jabłonków pass district and two mountain settlements, called Skalite and Cierne, the latter being a railroad junction.[156] Cadca remained in Czechoslovakia by mutual agreement.

The Polish-Czechoslovak frontier truce and mixed delimitation commissions were negotiated during the entire period beginning on October 1, 1938. A protocol was signed in Mistek, Czechoslovakia on October 23, 1938, concerning the Teschen-Silesian frontier. By November 30, 1938, all disturbances and territorial adjustments were to be completed. On December 10, orders came from Marshal Śmigły-Rydz to General Bortnowski to liquidate and evacuate the Śląsk army from Teschen. The Warsaw General Staff orders were carried out.[157]

CHAPTER THREE

THE FINAL DISMEMBERMENT OF CZECHOSLOVAKIA
OCTOBER 1938- MARCH 1939

In the wake of the Munich settlement Czechoslovakia evolved into a state that increasingly relied on the succor and direction of Hitler's Germany. This policy did not prevent Czechoslovakia from further partition and dissolution. In October 1938, Prague granted autonomy to Slovakia and the Carpatho-Ukraine after the Polish military occupation of Teschen.

At the same time Kálmán Kánya, the Hungarian foreign minister, congratulated Beck on uniting the Trans-Olza area with Poland, and through his Warsaw minister, Andreas de Hory, he requested that Poland should give no guarantees to Prague before Hungary also had a chance to present her demands against Czechoslovakia.[1] The Polish government answered that it would always take an active interest in what was happening in Czechoslovakia, and that Poland had a friendly attitude toward Hungarian territorial claims, and that Warsaw would never give any "guarantees" until Hungarian-Czech relations were finally regulated.[2]

On October 3, 1938, a note was sent by the Hungarians to Prague demanding "self-determination for the Magyars of Czechoslovakia on a basis identical with that adopted for the Germans." Budapest also sent the Hungarian *Chef de Cabinet,* Count Csáky, to Warsaw.[3]

The Hungarian diplomat informed Beck that Budapest had no intention of invading Slovakia or of opposing that nation's foreseen declaration of independence.[4] However, Csáky requested support for extensive Slovak frontier revision in favor of Hungary. The aim of the Hungarians was also to ask for direct Polish military assistance in occupying the easternmost province of Czechoslovakia, the Carpatho-Ukraine.[5] Beck told Csáky that Poland could not militarily help occupy the Carpatho-Ukraine for Hungary because of the "moral" principles involved. Nevertheless, the foreign minister promised Polish support for Hungarian irredenta.[6]

The Carpatho-Ukraine, a forgotten region of Europe, now became part of the international struggle stemming from Czech disintegration, as Professor Lukacs wrote:

There was (and is) a dark side of Europe, as there is a dark side of the moon. The distance between the Carpatho-Ukraine, and, say, Normandy was hardly less than that between Canterbury and the

Gobi Desert. The ignorance of the leading statesmen of the Western democracies regarding Eastern Europe was and remains inexcusable. Their ignorance regarding the Carpathian Ukraine at least was understandable. Yet, in a way, this province was the key to a great change in the entire Eurasian constellation of the Great Powers during the winter of 1938-39. I must sketch its complex situation as briefly as possible.

Between the wars the Ukrainian people lived under three sovereignties. The large majority continued to live within the Soviet Union. After World War I 3½ million Ukrainians found themselves within the confines of the new Polish state, for which they professed little or no loyalty. Finally there were another 600,000 in the easternmost province of Czechoslovakia, separated from their brethren to the northeast by the Carpathian Mountains: hence the name Carpatho-Ukraine. It was a dark, muddy, mountainous province, superstitious and backward, light-years away not only from Western Europe, but also light-months behind the neon-lit shopfronts of Prague. Its inhabitants, unlike many of the Ukrainians within Poland, had never lived under the sovereignty of the Russian Empire. Before 1918 they belonged to the kingdom of Hungary— indeed, there was a considerable sprinkling of Hungarians within the Carpathian Ukraine. Now, in 1938, they became excited during the dissolution of Czechoslovakia.[7]

In this period, Hungarian special units were organized to conduct military diversion and anti-Czech propaganda in the Carpatho-Ukraine. The use of irregular troops by Budapest had a long tradition in Hungarian post-Treaty of Trianon policies. This active irredentist movement was almost always directly controlled by the Hungarian army.[8]

Meanwhile, Czechoslovakia's post-Munich position as a viable state continued to deteriorate. On October 11, 1938, Prague officially created an autonomous Carpatho-Ukrainian government.[9] This internal change was preceded by the Slovaks who demanded and got from the Czechs an autonomous Slovakia on October 6.

From the beginning the newly-created Carpatho-Ukrainian government became an arena of conflicting interests. The political approach of the government was divided between a Ukrainian intellectual and cultural orientation versus a Great Russian one.[10]

The political changes in the Carpatho-Ukraine were closely observed and monitored by Hitler's Germany. On October 7, in a series of foreign notes, it was recommended that Germany use the Carpatho-Ukraine area as a spring board for bringing about a future Greater Ukraine.[11] German aid to the Ukrainian organizations was extensive and known to Hitler. The German chancellor hoped to use the Carpatho-Ukraine as base for a plan to bring peace to Central Europe. This, in Ukrainian eyes, would create a new partition of Poland, with Germany seizing Danzig and Upper Silesia. According to the Polish intelligence reports, Western Galicia would unite with the Russian Ukraine.[12]

The Ukrainian movement in Germany was divided into two general groups: the old Hetman group of Pavlo Skoropadsky, and the more important nationalist movement *O.U.N.* (*Objednannia Ukrainskych Nacjonalistiw.*) It was the *O.U.N.* organization that received the most German aid, although the Skoropadsky movement was used as a propaganda and diversionary organization directed against Poland. Throughout the first months of 1938 talks took place between the German authorities and the Ukrainian nationalists. In April 1938, a united organization was formed called *Verband der Ukrainer in Gross Deutschland*, made up of Ukrainians who had German citizenship. Ukrainians who were emigrés or who had other citizenship were urged to join *U.N.O.* (*Ukrainska Narodna Obnowa*), with headquarters in Berlin.[13] The *U.N.O.* organization also had centers in Bremen, Vienna, Danzig, Gabel, Havellan, Grimmen, Reichenberg, Brix, Aussig, and Leitmeritz.[14]

In May 1938 in Bremen and Delmenhorst, a Ukrainian Legion was organized in order to create a trained military cadre prepared to go to Poland and the Carpatho-Ukraine. The training was supervised by a German SA *Stürmfuhrer* and the *Abwehr*. The money came from a Ukrainian organization in Czechoslovakia (*Ukrainisches Unabhängigkeitskomite*).[15] Also, secret and semi-secret research centers functioned in Germany that closely studied East Central Europe, its people, press, and books. Many of the printed periodicals were translated into German.[16] The Poles watched these centers very closely. The most important study centers were located in Breslau (Wrocław), *Ost Europa Institut*; Königsberg, *Ost Europa Verlag*; Berlin, *Ukrainisches Wissenshaftliches Institut*; and the University of Münster which specialized in Slavic languages, in particular the Ukrainian language. These institutes were usually associated with their respective universities. Königsberg specialized in studies directed toward the Soviet Union, while the Breslau institute concentrated on Poland and the Ukraine. The tone of these studies was not only anti-Polish, but also anti-Hungarian. The funding for these centers came directly and indirectly from government circles and from the German army.[17] The Ukrainian national movement was controlled by German army intelligence not only in Poland and the Carpatho-Ukraine, but also in the Soviet Union. The main coordinating center for the dispersing of funds and orders to the Ukrainian nationalists was the German consulate in the city of Cracow. Since the early

1930s Polish counter-intelligence managed secretly to intercept and photograph the bulk of the consulate's confidential correspondence with Germany and the Ukrainian nationalist movement.[18]

In these intelligence reports the Poles observed that at the height of the Carpatho-Ukrainian crisis, the governing circles of the Third Reich would be making a choice on future policy whether to recognize Polish interests in East Central Europe and work with Poland as a future neighbor of the Ukraine. The other tactic supported strongly by the German General Staff was the Ukrainian nationalist movement, which they aided in creating a "Greater Ukraine" with the cooperation of Rumania. This "Greater Ukraine" was to reach from Lviv (Lwów) to Kiev, and was to partition Poland and unite with the Russian Ukraine.[19]

While the fate of the Carpatho-Ukraine hung in the balance, Poland continued to do everything possible to bring about a common Polish-Hungarian border. For Warsaw this new boundary would strategically help break the hostile encirclement on her southern frontier. Poland also became increasingly alert to the growing German influence on her southeastern flank, and to the impact of a new Ukrainian state on Poland's large Ukrainian minority.[20]

As the situation in the Carpatho-Ukraine grew more tense, the Polish-Carpathian border was reinforced by units of the Polish Border Corps, *KOP*. At the same time, a press campaign was initiated by Warsaw to spotlight the new events in the Carpatho-Ukraine.[21]

The Hungarians likewise realized that their territorial demands against the Czech state were coming in direct conflict with German designs on post-Munich Czechoslovakia. German policy rejected any plans for a common Hungarian-Polish frontier, even though Budapest tried to explain its Carpatho-Ukraine policy in anti-Bolshevik terms.[22] The Poles, during October, also attempted to persuade Great Britain and France that a border with Hungary would stabilize that region of Eastern Europe, and that a barrier would be created not only against Soviet Russia, but also against Germany.[23]

However, Hungary increasingly began to shy away from independent action in the Carpatho-Ukraine, and started seeking German approval for a Hungarian-Polish border through Italian mediation. Beck immediately informed Budapest that turning toward the Munich Powers would not be regarded as desirable, and Warsaw might cease to be interested in any Hungarian territorial revindications.[24] In spite of Polish warnings Budapest was willing to make its relations more dependent on Germany.[25]

The failure of direct Czech-Hungarian negotiations conducted between October 9 and 13 brought about partial Hungarian mobilization to counter the already mobilized though rapidly disintegrating Czechoslovak army.

At the same time, Hungary sent a former prime minister, Kálmán Darányi, on a special mission seeking definite support from the German Führer.[26] Darányi's mission to Hitler and Budapest's early *demarches* toward Germany alarmed the Poles. Beck again warned, directly through his Budapest minister Orłowski, that Poland would discontinue its interest in Hungarian land claims if Budapest continued to rely on the Munich Powers.[27]

The Poles saw that independent Hungarian action was "escaping out of their hands," and at the same time increasing German influence was jeopardizing Warsaw's southern strategic position. Yet Beck still hoped that a Polish-Hungarian frontier could be created outside of German-Hungarian collusion. He tried to dispel Hungarian fears of Rumanian and Little Entente displeasure over the planned incorporation of the Carpatho-Ukraine. On October 15-18 Beck visited King Carol of Rumania and asked for Rumanian cooperation and consent for the annexation of the Carpatho-Ukraine by Hungary. He also promised Bucharest some territory out of the Ruthenian partition. The Rumanians told Beck that they desired better relations with Budapest, but they were cool towards any Hungarian territorial extension at the expense of Czechoslovakia.[28]

During the same time, Beck sent his *Chef de Cabinet*, Michał Lubieński, to Budapest, to stiffen Hungarian resolve not to appeal for German-Italian arbitration.[29] Furthermore, word was given to start Polish military diversionary operations to aid the Hungarians in the Carpatho-Ukrainian region. The organization and command was carried out by Polish intelligence.[30] The military activity was directed by intelligence section No. 2 (*Ekspozytura*,)which was first organized in 1930 for diversion in case of war. The section was headed by Major Edmund Charaszkiewicz. Polish intelligence also had for a long time operated extensively in Uzhgorod and Chust (Khust), the principal cities of the Carpatho-Ukraine.[31]

The personnel who were to take part in the military action were recruited by Polish intelligence secretly and with caution. The men were volunteer army reserve officers and university students who belonged to shooting clubs. Most had some knowledge of the Ukrainian language and were familiar with the general terrain.[32] These people were adequately armed by Polish intelligence and given orders to destroy bridges and police and army installations. They were informed that if captured they could not count on official Polish government support or aid. In order to not clash militarily with Hungarian forces which were simultaneously conducting military operations, code words were to be used.[33]

During this entire period Poland was exposed to regular Ukrainian language and propaganda broadcasts emanating from Germany. These radio stations located in Vienna, Graz, Leipzig, and Breslau brought about a high state of "excitement" among the Ukrainian population living in southeastern Poland. The broadcasts were "jammed" by Warsaw, and the Poles let Germany know that they were very sensitive on all questions connected with the Ukraine.[34]

On October 24, 1938, a series of high level German-Polish conversations were held in Berchtesgaden between the Polish ambassador Józef Lipski and the Reich foreign minister Joachim von Ribbentrop. It was revealed by Berlin that Polish independent participation in any Hungarian territorial revindication or arbitration was not looked on with favor by Germany. On the other hand, Herr von Ribbentrop told the ambassador that the time had arrived for a "total solution" of all outstanding issues between the two nations. Poland was invited to join the Anti-Comintern Pact. The Free City of Danzig would return to Germany, and an extraterritorial strip would be built through Polish Pomerania to connect East Prussia with Germany. In return, Poland would receive a 25-year extension of the Polish-German Non-Aggression Agreement and a guarantee of the Polish-German frontier.[35]

Meanwhile, German influence directly manifested itself in the Carpatho-Ukraine on October 25-26, when a new nationalistic Ukrainian regime headed by Monsignor Dr. Augustin Voloshyn took power from a pro-Hungarian government. The newly-formed Carpatho-Ukrainian armed forces were reorganized on the SA model. German-trained Ukrainian officers were also sent in by Berlin. The men were fitted with German grey uniforms and "Hitler-Jugend side-arms." The newly formed Carpatho-Ukrainian government was "established along Nazi lines" and other Ukrainian groups and political parties were outlawed.[36]

The Polish minister in Budapest, in a last-minute effort, tried again to persuade the Hungarians not to put their fate into any German-Italian official arbitration. But Hungary was no longer prepared to act independently with Warsaw on the Carpatho-Ukraine question, or in its claims to Southern Slovakia. The Hungarians told the Poles that the Ruthenian problem could only be solved by Berlin and that Germany had many outstanding problems to settle with Poland. According to Budapest, the Carpatho-Ukraine question was being used by Berlin as a bargaining point to put pressure on Hungary as well as Poland.[37] Orłowski criticized Hungarian diplomatic tactics, and reminded Foreign Minister Kánya that Germany could not be trusted. The Poles charged also that the Hungarian diplomatic initiative was no "longer in their hands," and Warsaw was embarrassed and pinioned by Hungarian policy. Kánya, in a "depressed" mood, answered that he hoped to avoid Rumanian mobilization and war, and that diversionary activity in

Ruthenia did not bring about any real results. Orłowski stated that the Carpatho-Ukraine problem would not be settled due to the economic and political partition of the territory.[38]

After his conversation with Kánya, Orłowski visited the former Hungarian prime minister, Count István Bethlen. The elder statesman had a great influence over Hungarian policy and was a close confidant of Regent Horthy. Bethlen told Orłowski that Kánya made a mistake by not stating clearly the Hungarian position toward the Carpatho-Ukraine. Bethlen stated that Kánya tried to hide Budapest's true territorial intentions by claiming to demand ethnically Hungarian lands and not a common Polish-Hungarian frontier. Bethlen also revealed that Kánya would soon resign.[39]

The Poles saw that a joint Budapest-Warsaw démarche in eastern Czechoslovakia would not take place due to the dominant role of Berlin in Prague. To this state of affairs, Warsaw reacted by making new territorial demands from Slovakia in the mountainous pass area of Cadea-Zwardon and the Jaworina (Jaworzyna) area. The Polish officials told the Slovak representative informally that these border adjustments were of strategic importance to Poland. When the Slovaks asked "against whom," the Poles did not answer the question. The new Slovak regime informed the German government of Polish pressure and asked for support regarding the demarcation of the frontier.[40] On November 1 1938, the final negotiations between Prague and Warsaw began. The Slovak government also negotiated with Poland in the city of Bratislava the signing of a border agreement on November 30 in the Polish mountain resort of Zakopane.[41]

Throughout 1938 the German-Polish frontier was closed from the area of Schwednitz (Swidnica) in Silesia to the city of Stolp (Słupsk) in Pomerania. Almost the whole of East Prussia was considered a closed territory. The central frontier between the Polish border and Berlin was closed to foreign air traffic. A German eastern fortification line followed the river Oder from Oppeln (Opole) in the south to the city of Glogau (Głogów), and then northward to the river Noteć ending in a Pomeranian lake and forest belt.[42]

During the last days of October the German government initiated a massive deportation of Polish Jews who lived in Germany but had Polish passports. The reason for this deportation was that the Polish Ministry of the Interior, along with the Foreign Office, had issued a decree establishing new passport controls for people crossing the German-Polish frontier. The expulsion of Polish Jews surprised Polish circles. By the end of October over 17,000 Jews with Polish papers had been forced to leave Germany. These people for the most part had very little true contact with Poland proper. The majority of the Jews had left Polish territory before the First World War, or shortly thereafter. Their lack of basic knowledge of Polish culture and language enabled Berlin to press Poland on the matter of the Jews.[43] The Poles refused to step in line with Berlin on this Jewish question and Warsaw threatened retaliation by the expulsion of Germans and German Jews living in Poland, unless these Jews were permitted to return to Germany for a sufficient period of time to settle their financial affairs; Berlin agreed.[44]

Polish intelligence reported that these pogroms were centrally planned and directed, reaching high intensity after the assassination of a German diplomatic secretary in Paris by a German-Polish Jew on November 7, 1938. The German press called this act an open provocation by international Jewish circles. During the numerous acts of vandalism and murder which followed the police did very little to intervene, nor did the fire brigades put out fires on property owned by Jews. Polish intelligence observed that the German population did not react positively to the anti-Jewish brutality exemplified by the Nazis.[45]

The first Vienna Arbitration, on November 1, 1938, carried out by Germany and Italy, sanctioning the partition of the Carpatho-Ukraine, did not satisfy Hungarian claims or protect the new semi-autonomous Carpatho-Ukrainian state against active Hungarian irredentism.[46] The Carpatho-Ukrainian government did not formally protest the Vienna Award, but on November 3-4, 1938, it issued a series of statements manifesting its discontent. Monsignor Voloshyn, the Carpatho-Ukrainian prime minister, and his Central Ukrainian National Council issued the following statements:

The tearing away of our ancient cities, Uzhhorod and Mukachiv, from the Carpatho-Ukraine is a wound to our Fatherland. But at this important moment we must remember this: that at the price of our wounds the independence of the Ukrainian nation has been obtained. This heavy blow which met us will not shake our will to accomplish that great task which history has destined for us . . . We have decided to begin the historical task of building up our severed but independent country . . . God will help us to fulfull our historical task.[47]

The Ukrainian Council appealed to the Carpatho-Ukrainian people that:

this bad news should not cause desperation among the patriots.

Times will come when the whole nation of ours will unite in one
united sovereign State.

At the same time, we let you know with great joy that the frontiers
of our Sub-Carpathian State now are guaranteed by Germany, Italy,
England and France. Poland and Hungary accepted the (Vienna)
award and took upon themselves an obligation not to interfere with
our internal affairs.[48]

Hungary amid national "pomp and ceremony" quickly occupied the
awarded territories in pre-arranged stages between November 3 and 8.[49]
During the same week, on November 3, the Polish minister in Budapest,
Leon Orłowski, handed a letter to Regent Horthy from President Mościcki.[50] The Hungarian regent told the Polish minister that at present
the annexation of Ruthenia to Hungary "was mathematical" (i.e. logically inescapable). Orłowski expressed agreement with this view, and
when Horthy asked for his opinion as to the future of the Carpatho-
Ukrainian question, the Polish minister answered that Hungarian policy
should follow three directions: that of preventing German-Italian
guarantees of the present territories of Czechoslovakia, that of exerting
economic pressure on the rest of the Carpatho-Ukraine, and that of
continuing military action in that region. The Hungarian regent remained
silent.[51] Orłowski reported to Warsaw that it was his impression that
the Hungarian government intended to continue its military activities
in Ruthenia.[52]

On November 4 Polish Foreign Minister Beck held a conference at
his ministry.[53] It was the consensus of the gathering that the League
of Nations was no longer a viable international institution and that
France's East European system had been compromised by the events
in post-Munich Czechoslovakia. The Czechoslovak state had shown its
internal weaknesses: military disarray and national disunity. Warsaw
saw in Czechoslovakia's acquiescence to German demands a rare example
of the complete political and psychological breakdown of a nation;
"without a single shot" it had permitted the reorganization of its territory by foreign powers. Great Britain and France had shown a "complete
disinterest" in the Vienna Award. Italy had backed a common Polish-
Hungarian frontier far beyond the expectations of the Poles.[54] It was
also observed that recent events had increased German suspicions regarding
Polish plans in the Carpatho-Ukraine. The possibility of Stalin's sudden
death was judged to be "catastrophic," as Germany would then strongly
press its Ukrainian policy.[55]

Three days after Beck's conference, on November 7, the Polish Foreign
Ministry received dispatches from Minister Orłowski in Budapest stating

in effect that Germany would not permit further Hungarian territorial expansion at the expense of the Carpatho-Ukraine because such action would discredit the recent Vienna Arbitration. According to Orłowski a "panic" fear of Germany reigned in the Hungarian Foreign Office.[56]

On November 8, Foreign Minister Beck told the German ambassador to Warsaw, Hans Adolf von Moltke, that "he did not consider the rump area of the Carpatho-Ukraine, in which there were no cities and railways, as viable. He therefore assumed that the population would on its own initiative, and in the very near future, express a desire for a plebiscite."[57]

On November 9 Hungary, through its Minister Andreas de Hory, turned again to Warsaw asking for continued Polish covert military activity in Ruthenia.[58] Through the minister to Warsaw, Budapest informed Beck that expanded Polish military aid would facilitate a truly independent Hungarian policy that would not lean on other interested powers.[59]

The Hungarians asked for overt Polish military aid. Budapest searched for a formula which would bring direct Polish intervention into Ruthenia. Hungary presented a series of occupation plans which would entail overt Polish-Hungarian military collaboration. The Hungarian General Staff requested the Polish General Staff "to engage four battle divisions of the regular Polish army in the occupation of the northern Carpatho-Ukraine." The Polish military leaders flatly rejected the Hungarian proposals.[60] However, Minister Beck told Budapest that Poland would continue her military support to Hungary in the Carpatho-Ukraine and gave assurances that Rumania would not pose a military threat to Hungary.[61]

Beck told the Hungarian minister to Warsaw, de Hory, that a common Hungarian-Polish border was of prime importance to both nations. In Beck's opinion, Hungary could have an independent policy only if she based it on the support of Poland, which had no conflicts of interest with Hungary. Furthermore, he stated that sooner or later Budapest must make an orientation choice in her relations with Germany.[62]

The Hungarian government continued to press its case for annexation of the Carpatho-Ukraine with the Axis. The Hungarian minister in Rome "hinted at the possibility of disorders in Ruthenia." Horthy in Budapest informed the German minister, Otto von Erdmannsdorff, that he was "worried over the problem of the Carpatho-Ukraine. The Hungarian Government was being besieged with requests to put an end to the untenable conditions there."[63] The German Foreign Ministry in a series of confidential reports began to note its fear of a *fait accompli* in the Carpatho-Ukraine. The director of the political department of the German

Foreign Ministry, Ernst Woermann, on November 12, 1938, proposed to Foreign Minister von Ribbentrop that Germany seek an immediate exchange of views with the Italian government, whose views to date had been "at least uncertain"; that Germany and Italy demand that Hungary respect the Vienna Award and suppress any subversive activity; that Germany discount "a similar *démarche* with the Polish Government . . . on account of the connection with other pending questions"; that the question of a German-Italian guarantee to Czechoslovakia be examined in this connection; and that, as a German counteraction against the Polish agitation, Germany promptly give financial support to the remaining Carpatho-Ukrainian territory.[64]

Britain's ambassador to Warsaw, Sir Howard Kennard, dispatched to his superior, Viscount Halifax, on November 14, 1938, his appraisal of the Polish position. "The Polish Government," he wrote, "still do not accept the Vienna arbitration as final but will endeavour to bring about in the near future a common frontier with Hungary. Their real motives are fear of Ukraine agitation and German penetration towards the Ukraine via Czechoslovakia."[65]

The Italian government warned Budapest that any revolt or open military intervention in the Carpatho-Ukraine would be opposed by Germany, and that Italy would have to support the Axis decision that had been made in Vienna. Nevertheless the Hungarian military and the Ragged Guard paramilitary organization continued to plan a military-led coup in Ruthenia and pressed the government for direct action.[66]

During this period there was a constant press campaign emanating from Poland, openly critical of the Vienna Award and demanding a common border with Hungary. On November 14, Horthy told the German minister Erdmannsdorff that the Ruthenian area was economically very close to Hungary and that a Polish-Hungarian bloc was not what mattered for Germany. He also stated that the natural topography (deep north-south mountain valleys) of the Carpatho-Ukraine would only hamper German plans for using the area as a springboard towards the Ukraine.[67]

On November 18, the Hungarian government stated to Berlin that the situation in the Carpatho-Ukraine was beginning to be untenable and that it was difficult for the Hungarians to continue to exercise restraint. At the same time, however, Budapest made it clear that it was anxious to confer with Berlin over the question of using military force in the Carpatho-Ukraine. The German government warned Hungary not to take any action in Ruthenia as envisaged by Regent Horthy. Berlin cautioned that Hungarian action would give rise to difficulties with Czechoslovakia and that Germany would not support Budapest.[68]

On November 19, at the height of the Carpatho-Ukrainian crisis, Poland's ambassador to Berlin, Józef Lipski, held his first meeting since October 24 with Foreign Minister Joachim von Ribbentrop.[69] Lipski communicated Beck's answer concerning the Danzig question, "that any tendency to incorporate the Free City into the Reich must inevitably lead to a conflict, not of a local character only, but one also jeopardizing Polish-German relations in the entirety." The German foreign minister replied that he regretted the position taken by Foreign Minister Beck. Ribbentrop suggested that:

> a long-term solution of the German-Polish problem by which Danzig would go to Germany might well result in domestic political difficulties for M. Beck, but on the other hand it should not be forgotten that the Führer would not find it easy either to justify to the German people a guarantee of the Polish Corridor.[70]

The German foreign minister told Lipski that he was "very much surprised that such a solution as the Führer had in mind could endanger German-Polish relations." He suggested that the talks of October 24 had been held "with the intention of placing German-Polish relations on an absolutely permanent basis and eliminating all imaginable points of friction," by implication including Hungarian-Polish interests in the Carpatho-Ukraine which had been a topic of discussion on October 24.[71]

On November 21 a strong note was presented to Budapest jointly by Germany and Italy, demanding the cessation of Hungarian military incursion into the Carpatho-Ukraine. The Axis Powers reminded Hungary that the Vienna Agreement, under which Germany and Italy had set the boundary between Hungary and the Carpatho-Ukraine, had been signed by Hungary, who had thus accepted this boundary. Hungarian military activity in the Carpatho-Ukraine would place the former morally "in a very difficult position"; moreover, it would "render valueless the Vienna Award to the discredit of the two arbitrating powers."[72] The German-Italian note was received by the Hungarian foreign minister with disappointment and excitement. The meeting ended in a "very heated" conversation with German Minister Erdmannsdorff.[73]

That same evening Kánya called Minister Orłowski to inform him, in a "dispirited manner," that the Hungarian invasion of the Carpatho-Ukraine was called off because of the Axis démarche. Kánya showed the German-Italian notes to Orłowski. The Hungarian foreign minister assured Orłowski that Budapest would continue to be interested in the Carpatho-Ukraine, but that now Kánya would work for a "plebiscite" in the area. Orłowski

reported that Kánya's "twists" and "delays" had made him a victim of
his own policy.[74]

Hungary was apparently by now coming to the conclusion that in order
to achieve her ends in Central Europe, she would have to follow
Germany's lead. Through her minister in Berlin, Sztójay, she informed
Germany that she wanted closer relations with the Axis Powers and that
she was prepared to join the Anti-Comintern Pact. Ribbentrop told Sztójay that Germany would not permit anyone to "predetermine her course
of action" and was concerned about the manner in which Hungarian
diplomacy was being conducted "via Rome." The Hungarian minister
nevertheless asked whether the German government could disinterest
itself from the problem of Hungarian interest in the Carpatho-Ukraine.
Ribbentrop replied that the answer had already been given in advance
through the note delivered in Budapest. He also warned the Hungarians
not to take any action without the support of Berlin.[75]

On November 22, Beck, in a conversation with Szembek, declared
that Poland had lost the opportunity of bringing about a common border
with Hungary. He blamed Kánya and the Hungarian government for a
cowardly and double-dealing policy and regretted that Budapest had not
taken advantage of opportunities presented to her in the Carpatho-
Ukraine. Beck said he did not foresee any changes in German policy
towards Poland because of the Ruthenian crisis, but that negative relations
between Germany and Poland had developed over the Carpatho-Ukraine
question.[76]

On the same day, Beck received the German ambassador, von Moltke,
to discuss the German-Italian note which had been sent to Budapest.
Von Moltke stated that since the Polish government supported the Hungarian claims in the Carpatho-Ukraine, Germany hoped that now Poland
would exercise her influence in the direction of the Axis Powers. Von
Moltke obtained Beck's assurance that Warsaw would attempt to still
the pro-Hungarian Polish press campaign. The German ambassador dismissed Beck's references to the desire of the Carpatho-Ukrainians for
union with Hungary as Hungarian propaganda. Beck said that he regretted
the continued unsettled situation there. He asked whether Germany had
any fundamental objections to the common Polish-Hungarian frontier.
Moltke answered that Germany refused to overthrow immediately an
award which had just been made and was recognized by all parties:
fundamental objections to the common frontier were not involved in this
attitude.[77]

On November 24, indecisive on means to be used by Hungary in futher-
ing her policies in the Carpatho-Ukraine, Regent Horthy told the German

Minister to Budapest that Italy had not warned Hungary against marching into the Carpatho-Ukraine, but had only pointed out that Berlin might possibly be opposed to this, and in that event, Italy could not do other than associate herself with a possible German protest. The regent also stated that the German intervention had made a "painful impression" on Hungary. He added that, as time went on, the instability of the remainder of the Carpatho-Ukraine would become more and more evident.[78]

The November failure of Hungarian policy in the Carpatho-Ukraine brought about a parliamentary crisis which caused the fall of Béla Imrédy's government. Regent Horthy refused to accept Imrédy's resignation, but Foreign Minister Kálmán Kánya was replaced by his *Chef de Cabinet* Count Csáky on November 28.[79]

Polish intelligence evaluated the current political situation. On November 29, Major Jan Lésniak, chief of the "Western" German section of Polish intelligence, delivered a "top secret" lecture to the higher commanders of the Polish army outside of Warsaw. He stated that the general situation in Europe in 1938 had brought about an unusual territorial expansion of German power, under the leadership of Hitler.[80]

The Austrian success strengthened the German position on the Danube and in Hungary. Berlin's road to economic expansion into the southeast was set. Thus, the Austrian *Anschluss* created the Sudeten crisis. Besides the strong anti-war sentiment of the German people, two elements had played a key role: the change in organization and personnel in the army and *ancien régime* leadership during 1938, and the continued intensive growth of the armed forces to over 1,200,000 men.[81] The Austrian-Sudeten military actions were characterized by:

1. Secret mobilization, concentration and preparation.
2. Speed of execution of military action.
3. Preparedness to meet all eventualities.
4. Extensive use of reserves.

The Austrian and Sudeten crises were very similar from the military standpoint. The Sudeten problem took much longer from the political (i.e. Munich Conference) point of view. In both cases the German army was prepared for military action if resistance was encountered.[82]

Polish-German relations remained officially the same within the confines of the 1934 Non-Aggression Pact. During the Austrian-Sudeten crisis there were no major political problems which would directly collide with Polish national interest, but German nationalism on the international level and foreign policy had become very developed and domineering. The German press had slightly toned down its anti-Polish attacks. Yet the situation of the Polish minority in Germany had not improved. The Danzig situation remained critical apart from the positive stands of the officials involved.[83]

The general Polish intelligence conclusions were:

1. The German political power situation had improved considerably in 1938.
2. Undoubtedly Germany was preparing in the near future to challenge and resolve the question of hegemony with the Western Powers.
3. German projected expansion into the southeast was in 1938 no longer completely clear.
4. The German colonial claims had been officially presented by Hitler.
5. It seemed that Germany had a growing interest in Russia as an object not as a partner.
6. Germany, apart from difficult economic problems, was extensively preparing for war.
7. The German people, because of the tempo of the 1938 events, were psychologically unprepared to wage war.[84]

Despite Polish-Hungarian diplomatic reversals, neither state was willing to give up the idea of establishing a common border. The Polish government continued to support Budapest during the following four months, increasingly taking the diplomatic initiative in order to counter the growing German power in Eastern Europe.

By December Warsaw realized that a negative turning point with Berlin had been reached. The Foreign Ministry was aware that the Polish people would not permit their government to follow the Czech example. By December 6, Józef Potocki, head of the Western section of the Foreign Office, told Beck to expect German demands for an extraterritorial highway linking Germany with East Prussia. Beck believed that high level Berlin-Warsaw conversations must take place immediately to break this fast-forming "impasse."[85]

Beck, through Ambassador Lipski, invited Ribbentrop to Warsaw.[86] By their initiative the Poles hoped to ease the growing tensions between the two nations. Warsaw did not want any *faits accomplis* in Danzig and wanted to let Berlin know that Polish policy was not pursuing an anti-German barrier against expansion into the Danube region. Beck told the German ambassador that a way was possible to "take into consideration the interests of both countries" based on the Piłsudski-Hitler agreement of 1934, which had "proved its worth."[87]

Japan, observing the growth of Polish-German tensions, came forward with the proposal of using its good offices, since Tokyo gave great weight to the stability of good relations between Poland and Germany. Beck did not agree or disagree to the Japanese initiative presented by Ambassador Sh. Sakoh. The Japanese ambassador left directly for Berlin after the conversation. The Japanese, through their Berlin representative, Ambassador H. Oshima, told the Poles that Hitler and Ribbentrop saw German economic penetration into the Ukraine as one of the most important aspects of German politics. This policy had a natural outcome in Berlin's support of Ukrainian activity. The realization of this plan would be actualized in two or three years, barring any surprises such as the death of Stalin or the collapse of the Soviet regime. Since the basis of this Ukrainian plan was economic, Germany did not care about small pieces of territory such as Eastern Little Poland (East Galicia). Berlin's plans were on a greater scale, involving large territories and sparsely populated lands. Berlin supported the Carpatho-Ukraine up to a certain point, but even greater help came from the Ukrainian world emigration. This emigré movement considered the Carpatho-Ukraine as only a first stage to create conditions for better organization and propaganda, ever aiming at the ultimate goal of a Greater Ukraine. To Germany the Carpatho-Ukraine was of no real economic or strategic interest, and Berlin was not prepared to invest materially in that region, which was of marginal interest to German plans. Berlin's major interest was to organize and control the whole anti-Soviet emigré movement. The Carpatho-Ukraine independence movement was in its original intentions never directed against Poland, but against Russia. Germany knew well that her Ukrainian plans could be realized if Poland took her side.

The Carpatho-Ukrainian movement could also be used by Germany against Poland to bring her in line and isolate her from any understanding with Soviet Russia, but this advantage was not being pressed by Hitler. The Japanese told the Poles that for the realization of this plan concrete Polish-German talks concerning this cooperation must take place, but that this must not be done at the last minute. The Japanese military attaché in Budapest and Prague also told the Polish representative in Budapest that a common border with Hungary was possible soon, if Poland would join the Anti-Comintern Pact as Budapest was planning to do.[88]

Throughout December frontier incidents took place in the newly-incorporated areas of Polish Teschen. Polish intelligence reported that these incidents were inspired by German political agitators.[89]

In Paris a routine intelligence conference took place in December 1938, between the Polish intelligence chief, Colonel Pełczyński, and his French counterpart, Colonel Gauche. The French asked if the occupation of Danzig by German non-regular troops would cause the Poles to expect French intervention and war. The Poles answered that in their military planning Danzig incidents were considered an elementary basis for war with Germany and that Warsaw expected French aid.[90]

The territorial history of Danzig and the Ukraine had a heavy impact on the Polish psyche, Beck understood the maxim of his mentor Pilsudski that the Danzig question was a gauge of Polish-German relations, and that the Ukriane-Russian problem was very complicated. Beck maintained that Poland should do everything to remain independent from the pressure of Germany and Japan, that she join in the invasion of Russia as a natural ally. From the historical point of view the Ukrainian question could be regarded as Germany's failure during the First World War to bring about a modern Ukraine, and Poland's attempt at the same policy in 1920. According to the Polish foreign minister, Poland should "coexist" with the Soviet Union and give Moscow no reason to distrust its policy, although the historical danger of an understanding between Moscow and Berlin at the expense of Poland was always present.[91]

On December 20, 1938, Beck informed the German ambassador in Warsaw, von Moltke, that he would like to have a general discussion with Hitler and Ribbentrop before the German foreign minister's visit to Warsaw. Ribbentrop agreed.[92] Two conversations took place at Berchtesgaden on January 5 with Hitler, and continued in Munich with Ribbentrop the next day. The Germans stated they wanted a strong Poland and all existing misunderstandings should be eliminated. Hitler stressed that the danger came from Russia, "Bolshevist or Czarist," and that Poland's position should be preserved because its army saved Germany additional military expenditure, but he added that a definitive settlement must take place for Germany. This would mean the return of Danzig with a direct connection between East Prussia and Germany through the Polish Corridor, although Hitler assured Beck there would be no *fait accompli* engineered in the Free City. Beck received these statements with pessimism even when Hitler let him know that "Poland did not have the slightest thing to fear from Germany" in respect to the Ukraine. Berlin had wide-ranging economic interests and "Germany had no interests beyond the Carpathians and it was a matter of indifference to her what the countries interested in those areas did there."[93]

The conversations became more specific the following day in Munich. Beck informed Ribbentrop that he was concerned that Polish rights in Danzig might be affected in the near future, because in the minds of the Polish people and Piłsudski, "Danzig represented a touchstone of German-Polish relations." Ribbentrop again reiterated what Hitler stated by saying Germany desired "a definitive, comprehensive, and generous consolidation of mutual relations." The German foreign minister assured Beck that:

> . . . we were interested in the Soviet-Russian Ukraine only to the extent that we inflicted damage on Russia everywhere we could, just as she did on us; therefore we naturally kept up constant relations with the Russian Ukraine. But we had never operated in any way with the Polish Ukrainians; this had always been strictly avoided. The Führer had explained our negative attitude regarding a Greater Ukraine. The evil seemed to me to lie in the fact that naturally anti-Russian agitation in the Ukraine always had certain effects on the Polish minority and the Ukrainians in the Carpatho-Ukraine. In my opinion, however, this could be changed only if Poland and we would work together in every respect in the Ukrainian question. I could imagine that in the course of a general, generous settlement of all problems between Poland and us we might very well be moved to regard the Ukrainian question as covered by a special Polish prerogative and to support Poland in every way in dealing with this question. On the other hand, of course, this presupposed a more and more pronounced anti-Russian attitude on the part of Poland, since otherwise there would be no question of any mutual interest.[94]

Ribbentrop asked if Poland would accede to the Anti-Comintern Pact in the near future. Beck said that this was not possible at the present time.[95] The German minister again raised the Ukrainian issue of whether Poland had given up Piłsudski's eastern aspirations; Beck "laughingly" answered "that they had been in Kiev, and that these aspirations were doubtless still alive today."[96] The talks were to continue during Ribbentrop's visit to Warsaw between January 25 and 27.

The Warsaw conversations were held in a tense atmosphere although both sides tried to portray an attitude of accommodation and friendship.[97] The German minister again brought up the question of Danzig and an extraterritorial road and railway connection in return for guarantee of the German-Polish frontier and a recognition of Polish economic rights in Danzig. Beck said he could not view this matter with optimism. Ribbentrop once more brought up the question of coordinating policy towards the Soviet Union and the Ukraine. Beck answered that it was "no secret" that "Poland had aspirations toward the Soviet Ukraine," but the Polish minister pointed to the dangers that would arise from a "treaty with Germany directed against the Soviet Union." Beck gave Ribbentrop his opinion of the future of Russia: that Russia under internal pressure would drive to war was unlikely; that only if the Soviet Union would break into national states would the Ukraine problem become real, which was still a question of the future; thus the status quo would prevail. Ribbentrop stated that the Reich was ready to go hand in hand with Poland on the first two eventualities.[98] The German foreign minister condemned the passivity of Beck and stated that Poland would only gain in security by joining the Anti-Comintern powers.

The German-Polish talks convinced Berlin that all hope of enlisting Polish support in an eastern adventure was becoming futile, and a change of policy was a necessity.[99] The historian J. Lukacs observed that:

Sometime in January 1939 Stalin . . . began to change his course—and, perhaps, his mind. For one thing, Stalin began to slow down the purges and eventually put an end to them. For another, he was obssessed with the age-old Russian, and specifically Bolshevik, idea that the Western European bourgeois states, and specifically England, were willing to buy peace from Hitler at the expense of Russia. Stalin would not let this happen, come what may. Soon there were straws in the wind that this was not what Hitler had in his mind either. The best clue we have for tracing this development is through the Carpathian Ukraine. In the past (for the last time in 1936), Hitler had spoken about the German desire to get hold of the rich granary of the Ukraine. Much of this wish to expand Germany toward western Russia had been set down in *Mein Kampf*. Immediately before and after Munich, the Ukrainian nationalists in Central Europe were stirring into activity. Yet they received practically no support from Hitler. In the end he even allowed Hungary to occupy, and incorporate, the Carpatho-Ukraine into Hungary on 16 March 1939, when Czecho-Slovakia had fallen finally apart.

This was not lost on Stalin. He realized that the immediate key to his relationship with Germany was no longer the Ukraine, it was Poland . . . Whether Stalin was thinking in these terms as early as October 1938 we do not know. What we do know is evidence to the effect that he sought a better relationship with Hitler, long before the first significant contacts between the Soviet Union and the Third Reich began in April 1939. This relationship had to develop at the expense of Poland. Just as Austria was the key to the relationship of Germany and Italy, Poland was the key to that of Germany and

the Soviet Union... In the case of Poland it was a great relief
for Stalin to find that Hitler, *Mein Kampf* notwithstanding, would
forget the Ukrainians and the Ukraine, if need be.[100]

Thus, at the end of January, pressure on Warsaw increased, manifesting
itself in German-inspired agitation in Danzig, Eastern Poland, and the
Ukraine.[101] Border incidents took place. Hungary, at Poland's urging,
concentrated more troops on the Ruthenian frontier; the reason for
this was the proclamation by the Voloshyn government that it would
hold a single list election on February 12 to the First Carpatho-Ukrainian
Diet. Germany, in no uncertain terms, warned against any arbitrary
military action by Hungary. The Voloshyn government joined the Anti-
Comintern Pact during the elections.[102]

The Polish Foreign Ministry and Polish intelligence agreed that this
German-dominated "Greater Ukraine" movement must cease its activity.
A second broad organizational plan was put into operation with the
knowledge of Budapest.[103] This scheme had two parts: political
agitation (code word *preszowska*), using leaflets, organizing strikes
and demonstrations with the help of sympathetic people; and the
military activities, which had the code name *akcja z Ungvaru*. The
aim of the military section was to attack Ukrainian military posts,
barracks, government buildings, police stations, strategic bridges, and
rail communication. The Hungarians from the south continued similar
activity. The Ukrainian *Sitch* armed forces, for such a short period
of time, were well trained and disciplined by Ukrainian and German
officers. The higher *Sitch* ranks were made up of former Tsarist
officers and Ukrainian deserters from the Polish army, including
Ukrainian-speaking Germans.[104]

The German presence made itself apparent with the arrival of a German
consul to the new Carpatho-Ukraine capital of Khust on February 8.
At the end of February the deputy commander of the *Sitch* traveled
to Berlin to discuss the details of an agreement regarding the supply
of arms and ammunition by the *Wehrmacht*.[105] Budapest continued
to put out feelers through its military attaché to Germany concerning
the possibility of a march into Ruthenia, which should "not be taken"
by Berlin as political aggressiveness. The Hungarian Foreign Minister
Csáky, it was stated, had experienced domestic difficulty because of
the lack of Axis assistance which would make it difficult for him to
carry out the promised withdrawal of Hungary from the League of
Nations.[106]

While Polish-Hungarian pressure continued to be exerted on Ruthenia,
Beck hosted in Warsaw the Italian foreign minister, Count Galeazzo

Ciano, between February 25 and March 3. Both sides had come to the conclusion that Italy was not able to come to Poland's support. Ciano hoped that in time Poland would adopt a closer tie with Germany, as had Rome.[107] The Ciano-Beck meeting ended Axis reserve. The policy of sounding out Poland was over.

During the last days of February and the first weeks of March Hitler decided to encircle Poland and bring that state into his sphere, abandoning his larger eastern and Russian schemes for the time being.[108] Negotiations between the Czechs and Slovaks had broken down on March 9. Berlin exerted pressure on the Slovaks to proclaim their total independence from Prague and for the final dissolution of the Czech government of President Emil Hacha under the most brutal circumstances.[109]

On March 4, 1939, the Hungarians were already informed by Ribbentrop that they must be patient in their claims, but that he would inform Budapest if any development of interest should arise in the Czech question.[110] On March 11 a note was handed by the German representative to Budapest, Erdmannsdorff, giving German permission, under certain conditions, for the occupation of the Carpatho-Ukraine.[111] The Hungarians agreed, except for the chief of the Hungarian General Staff, General Henrik Werth. He asked for a few days, a "week at the latest," to begin military action, and stated that the Hungarian army "must reckon with Czech resistance." Erdmannsdorff and Gunther Altenburg, the head of the German Foreign Ministry political division, who arrived by plane from Berlin, stated on March 13 "with the greatest emphasis" that such a delay would be too late.[112]

Hungarian troops numbering 40,000 massed on the Ruthenian frontier on March 13, 1939. The next day they crossed the border, moving to the eastern border of Slovakia to seal off the country.[113] The Carpathian *Sitch* forces expected this attack; they began to disarm some of the Czech forces still in the region. An armed Czech-Ruthenian struggle ensued, which facilitated the Hungarian invasion. The Czech military forces under the command of General Lev Prchala were ordered not to turn over their arms to the *Sitch* forces.[114] Voloshyn sent a telegram through a Ukrainian delegation to the German consul at Khust to be sent to Berlin:

To the Foreign Minister, Berlin, Germany.
In the name of the Government of the Carpatho-Ukraine, I beg you to take cognizance of the declaration of our independence under the protection of the German Reich.

Prime Minister Dr. Volosin, Chust[115]

Voloshyn conveyed a message of explanation to Ribbentrop that "in view of the declaration of independence by Slovakia, it was impossible for the Ukrainian people to remain within the federative union of the Czechoslovak State."[116] The same day a special envoy of the new Ukrainian government reported to the German consul at Khust that Hungarian troops had crossed the Carpatho-Ukraine frontier, and military fire was reported in front of the German consul's office. The Voloshyn government also asked for German intervention to stop the Hungarian troop advance.[117] The Ukrainian telegrams remained unanswered by Berlin. Instructions were sent that "no action is to be taken" on the Voloshyn telegram.[118]

On the evening of March 14, Minister Voloshyn proclaimed the indpendence of the new state over the Khust radio station. The German Legation in Prague was notified of the Carpatho-Ukrianian declaration and again the Khust government asked for protection.[119] The Ukrainian government also sent a courier to the Rumanian border town of Sighet to send a telegram to Berlin. The wording of this telegram was similar to the previous appeals.[120]

State Secretary Ernst von Weizsäcker formulated on March 14, 1939, the official German justification that the Prague government "was neither willing nor able to guarantee a state of lasting peace" in Slovakia, which resulted in a declaration of Slovak independence by the Slovak Diet. The Carpatho-Ukraine, being in a state of "unrest and terror" with constant frontier incidents, was responsible for the Hungarian army advancing into Ruthenia to protect the Hungarian population.[121] Weizsäcker sent a "most urgent" telegram to the consulate at Khust to inform the Carpatho-Ukraine government that:

Hungarian troops having advanced against Carpatho-Ukraine on a broad front, the German Government advises it to offer no resistance. As matters stand, the German Government regrets that it is not in a position to assume the protectorate.[122]

After receiving the telegram from Berlin, the German Consul Hamilkar Hofmann went directly to the home of Minister Voloshyn where a number of Ukrainian leaders had gathered. The consul communicated the telegram from Berlin. This was the last official contact between the two governments.[123]

The Ruthenian capital of Khust was taken after some fighting by Hungarian troops on March 16, 1939. The *Sitch* forces fought a defensive action, retreating into the hills and high mountains. Those armed Ukrainians who did not surrender crossed the border into Slovakia or went back to Polish Galicia. Voloshyn and the remnant of his government as well as some *Sitch* troops crossed the Rumanian frontier as refugees. Hungarian military patrols in the "silent" snow of the mountains reached the Polish border on March 16. The Polish military forces, led by General Zygmunt Boruta-Spiechowicz, waited on the frontier and gave the Hungarians a "warm" welcome.[124]

The destruction of the Carpatho-Ukraine government by the establishment of a common Polish-Hungarian border brought to an end one of the most promising Ukrainian attempts at creating a Greater Ukraine during the inter-war period.[125]

CHAPTER FOUR

THE LAST SIX MONTHS:
MARCH-AUGUST 1939

The fall of Czechoslovakia was an imminent, but nevertheless strategic disaster for Poland; its terrain was now outflanked along the entire length of its southern frontier. A western attack on Poland could be launched from three directions: west, north and south. Furthermore, Warsaw's hopes of a friendly autonomous Slovakia on Poland's southern flank were dashed by the conclusion on March 23, 1939, of a German-Slovak treaty which put that new state under Reich protection.[1]

Warsaw expected all along that the Czech state would become neutral or more subservient to Germany, but the Poles did not expect Hitler to annex Bohemia and Moravia with such rapidity. Regarding the sought-after common border with Hungary, the Poles no longer saw it as an effective barrier against German eastward penetration, since Hungary was increasingly slipping into Germany's orbit.[2]

In contrast, the eastern frontier with Soviet Russia stretching from the Dniester River and the Rumanian border in the south as far as Latvia to the north was, except for a few official cross points, a closed border with a fresh-ploughed field area in front of a network of barbed wires, and a second-ploughed tract on the other side of the barbed-wire fence. Polish and Soviet military patrols observed the frontier with the use of dogs, watch towers, and sentries.[3] The Polish side of the frontier was manned by the special elite forces of *KOP*, originally organized in 1924 to secure the Polish-Soviet border. During the 1920s armed bands of fifteen to twenty-five people crisscrossed the frontier from the Soviet side, robbing the civilian population, attacking trains, and kidnapping regular Polish border guards. With the coming of the *KOP*, a strong reaction took place for every Bolshevik border encroachment. The Poles responded in kind, crossing the frontier, burning Soviet guard stations, and generally disrupting the Russian border regions. However, in a very short period of time these incidents decreased appreciably.[4]

The success of the *KOP*, which received better wages and living conditions than the regular army from a special budget of the Ministry of the Interior, created a demand for the expansion of this force. By 1939 the *KOP* was stationed on the Hungarian, Rumanian, Lithuanian, Latvian, East Prussian, and Soviet borders. The *KOP* possessed its own intelligence and counter-intelligence arm which was directed primarily against the Soviet Union. Its system on the Russian border had eight strategic outposts. All these centers were under the command of the regular central army intelligence centers located in Wilno (No. 1), with five northern *KOP* posts, and Lwów (No. 5), with five southern posts. The counterintelligence of the *KOP* was limited to the frontier regions.[5]

As a defensive measure in the southeastern borderlands, the Poles developed a mass flooding system based on the Dutch model of World War I. The construction of river earth dams, which when opened would cover approximately 20 kilometers in width and a distance of 200 kilometers, constituted this system. This flooding system was supported by the natural defensive advantage provided by the Pinsk marshes. The Polish government looked upon this project as a more economical and practical line of defense than a line of trenches or a "Maginot" line. The construction of this project was secret; the workmen were blindfolded before entering the work area, and again blindfolded before returning home. This flooding system was designed to serve as a defense against an invasion by Soviet ground forces and tanks, as well as to impede the effective transit of Soviet troops into Czechoslovak territory. In contrast, the Polish military authorities realized that no such natural barrier stood in the path of a possible invasion across the western frontier. The Polish-Soviet border had, beyond the long line of barbed-wire entanglements, a maintained forest belt about 20 kilometers within Poland, running north to south, used as a natural protective wall to hinder observation.[6]

Although the border was difficult to cross, smuggling from Poland to Russia was constant. There was traffic in scarce items such as women's clothing, silk stockings, cosmetics, and narcotics. In exchange the Poles received gold or Czarist gold rubles. The employment by Polish intelligence of smugglers was common, not only as a source of information but also as a means of sending in agents.[7] The use of official Soviet railroad transit was difficult and highly dangerous. Polish agents crossing the border legally or crossing the "green" Russian border had a 90 percent chance of being captured or exposed. Travel within Soviet Russia was an uncommon occurrence; only people who were on official business or who had police permission and proper documents could traverse Russia. Thus, anyone extensively traveling within the Soviet state was bound to be noted by the authorities.[8] Foreign workers and technicians coming out of Russia were regularly interviewed by Polish intelligence, and at times they provided a good source of information on Soviet industry and the military.[9] Polish intelligence took the Soviet threat very seriously. Half of its budget was devoted to the East, and its work was much more difficult than that directed against the Reich. The German nation, even under the domination of the Nazi party, was a much more open society than that of Soviet Russia.

Soviet espionage against Poland was very extensive. Over 300 agents were captured yearly by Polish counter-intelligence; out of this figure, ten cases were considered serious. Soviet espionage working in Poland was on two levels, encompassing the entire country. The first level was the NKVD (*Narodnyi Kommissariat Vnutrennykh Del*), which included diplomatic posts and agents in the field. A second espionage network functioning in Poland was directed by GRU Army Intelligence. The work for Polish counter-intelligence was doubly difficult because many of the Soviet agents were not only well trained, but were ideologically motivated.[10]

Polish "deep" espionage against Soviet Russia was directly controlled by Warsaw. All of the Russian land mass was covered with a system of couriers and a radio network stretching from the Polish border to Minsk, Leningrad, Kiev, and Moscow, and then across Russia to Murmansk. Poland also had radio communication centers bordering Russia in Mukden, Harbin, Tokyo, Kabul, Tehran, and Ankara.[11] The radio contact was kept to a minimum within Russia because of the danger of the radio transmitters being captured by Soviet authorities. The major method by which information was passed was agent couriers and normal diplomatic channels.

The main Polish radio receiving station for both east and west was located in a complex of camouflaged buildings in a forest outside of Warsaw in the area of Pyry. This 20-kilowatt center had radio antennae that could be raised and lowered automatically.[12] The Pyry communication center had the technology to change quickly from one wave to ten waves. Its studios could broadcast propaganda, code, orders, or ciphered texts.[13] The Poles also had radio listening stations located on the Soviet frontier in the northeast in the town of Lida, in the center at the city of Rowne, and in the southeast between Soviet Russia, Rumania, and Slovakia in the town of Kolomyja.[14]

Polish cryptologists had a thorough knowledge of Soviet military codes, which were not as complicated as the German military cipher system.[15] In contrast, the codes used by the Poles were called "peaceful" garrison codes, and were different for the army, navy and air force. In case of the outbreak of war a new code system would be introduced with special new cipher machines produced by Poland. Warsaw, being familiar with the German system, believed that these new Polish code machines were the most advanced in the world and "theoretically unbreakable," even if one of the machines was captured by the enemy. The Poles produced 125 machines, which in time of war were to be given by intelligence to the major army groups, the General Staff, military attachés, and intelligence centers.[16]

Polish intelligence in the east had for years also semi-secretly supported the nationalist movement of the non-Russian peoples within Soviet Russia. This movement, named after the Greek mythological figure Prometheus, had as its purpose to organize the non-Russian political emigration of Byelo-Russians, Tartars, Cossacks, Georgians, Armenians, Caucasians, Ukrainians, Azerbaijanis, and others into a common front, a joint conspiratorial alliance and political action. The Promethean concept was based on the theory that the post-World War I revolution in Eastern Europe from which Soviet Russia emerged was still an unfinished process. The followers of this movement hoped that the nationalist dynamism unleashed by the Great War would in time dissolve the Soviet state and the non-Russian nations would merge in the west with the Ukraine, Byelo-Russia and the Baltic peoples. A union of Turkic-Mohammedan states would emerge in the southeast; a Siberian union would appear in the east. The Polish General Staff gave extensive military training to officers from Georgia, the Ukraine, the Caucasus, and the Baltic state of Estonia. Although certain people within Polish intelligence and politics supported the Promethean movement, it did not have the complete favor of the last chief of Polish Intelligence, Józef Smoleński, or of Marshall Rydz-Śmigły. The performance of this movement and the funds that were spent did not bring the expected outcome within Soviet Russia.[17]

The intelligence achievements in the east, although taking at times more than half of the Second Department budget, did not bring forth the same type of results as intelligence work directed against Germany. This brought about a degree of suspicion and jealousy between the head of the Eastern Section, Captain Jerzy Wraga-Niezbrzycki, and the chief of Intelligence Center No. 3 at Bydgoszcz, Major Jan Żychoń. Niezbrzycki used his political contacts and charged that Żychoń's success in intercepting German documents was in reality a German plant.[18]

By the middle of March Warsaw again experienced a new diplomatic *démarche,* at first in a series of conversations between Lipski and Göring over Slovakia. That new state was partially occupied by the German army which was a "surprise" to Warsaw and made a "bad impression."[19] German troops entered Slovakia between March 15 and 27 and occupied a belt of land from Bratislava north to the Polish frontier, as well as the entire border between Slovakia and Poland from Teschen Silesia running along the Carpathian mountains to the Hungarian frontier. They began to build roads, erect fortifications, and garrison the territory. This was done with *fait accompli* methods.[20]

On March 20, Lipski arrived in Warsaw where he was met with a demonstration against Beck's "pro-German" policy. Lipski was pessimistic as to future Polish-German relations and he offered his resignation, which was refused. He returned to Berlin after receiving a telephone message that Ribbentrop had asked for a conversation. Beck told him that contacts had been made between Ambassador Raczyński and the British Foreign Office since the New Year and that he planned to visit London.[21] The Lipski-Ribbentrop talks were a continuation of the propositions of the past that Poland ally itself to Germany. The German minister stated that the Carpatho-Ukraine question was settled to Poland's satisfaction, and when Lipski stated that the news "hit Poland hard" when Berlin assumed the protection of Slovakia, Ribbentrop hinted that the Slovak question could be the subject of joint discussions "if German-Polish relations in general develop satisfactorily." The German minister stated that the "peculiar attitude" of Warsaw and the "stiffening" of Polish-German relations must end. He told Lipski that Beck should visit Hitler again for a general discussion, and a fresh attempt should be made to improve relations. Ribbentrop pointed out that Germany historically had her share in the creation and existence of Poland:

. . . If at Brest Litovsk, for example, Germany had pursued a different policy with Russia, there would be no Poland today. Under the Schleicher Government too, there had been the possibility that a Marxist Germany would ally herself with the Soviet Union. In that case too, Poland would hardly exist today. The basis on which German-Polish understanding could rest would only be provided by German and Polish nationalists, Poland must realize clearly that she could not take a middle course. Either Poland would remain a national State, working for a reasonable relationship with Germany and her Führer, or one day there would arise a Marxist Polish Government, which would then be absorbed by Bolshevist Russia.[22]

He stated that Berlin honestly desired a strong national Polish government under the Piłsudski colonels. However, in Ribbentrop's opinion, Poland must understand that her geographic position was indebted to Germany losing the war. According to him, it was Hitler who understood Poland's rights to the sea, but the condition was that Danzig return to the Reich and that extra-territorial rail and road connections be established across the "corridor" to East Prussia, in return for a German guarantee of the "corridor." In such circumstances Berlin was ready to deal with the Slovak question to every party's satisfaction. Germany, in treating the Ukrainian question in the past, had proved how loyal Berlin's attitude had been. Germany was prepared to regard the Ukrainian question from a purely Polish angle. A common German-Polish policy could become "very fruitful" in the future. However, a "juncture" had appeared in Polish-German relations. Ribbentrop stated that ". . . the Führer had felt nothing but amazement over Poland's strange attitude on a number of questions; it was important that he should not form the impression that Poland simply was not willing." After these talks Lipski left again for Warsaw to confer with Beck.[23]

During this time, on March 22, the Lithuanian government was forced to cede the Baltic port city of Klaipeda (Memel) to the Reich. The Memel takeover was militarily similar in method to the Czech crisis. Lithuania yielded.[24]

Lipski returned to Warsaw in the midst of the Memel takeover. His reports were very pessimistic. Szembek, in a conversation with Michał Lubieński, Beck's *Chef de Cabinet,* stated that it was time "to show the Germans our teeth." Poland would not give in on Danzig, because if Warsaw agreed to German guarantees which were of no value, as shown from past experience, she would "mechanically" be presented with further German demands.[25]

On March 23 Poland, in secret, mobilized four infantry divisions and one cavalry brigade, and strengthened the border with Germany in the areas of Pomerania, Poznań, Łódź, Cracow, and north of Warsaw. After the mobilization two extra divisions and one brigade of cavalry from the east were stationed on the German frontier.[26] The new chief of Polish Intelligence, Colonel Józef Smoleński, who replaced Colonel Tadeusz Pełczyński, called the Soviet military attaché in Warsaw to inform him that the March mobilization was not directed against Soviet Russia. The Soviet military attaché, Ribalko, stated that he was well aware of this.[27]

Polish war plans going back to the 1920s foresaw Soviet Russia as the main protagonist. This war design project was completed in the first part of 1939. The concept of the eastern enemy as the most dangerous stemmed from the ideas of Marshal Piłsudski. According to him, in a war with Soviet Russia, Poland would be alone with little or no aid coming from the West. But in a military engagement with Germany, Warsaw could count on France and her western and eastern allies. This Piłsudski view remained at the core of Polish military planning.[28] The Soviet thrust was projected to come in two wings: the northern wing near Wilno and the southern wing in the area of Lwów, bypassing the central marshes (Polesie), driving directly at Warsaw. The Polish plan was to cut this drive in parts as it moved inland. This mobile doctrine was based on the experiences of the Russo-Polish war of 1919-1920.[29]

Warsaw projected that the main German attack on Poland was to come from the northwest with two secondary thrusts from Silesia and East Prussia driving towards Warsaw. The Polish plan was to group three armies: one in front of Warsaw, a second army in the north against East Prussia and a southern army protecting the south in the Silesian-Łódź area. This defense strategy was based on the military support of France in the west.[30]

On the German-Polish border Berlin had the strategic advantage. The Versailles Treaty permitted Berlin to man and expand fortifications in East Prussia, while this was not permitted in Germany proper. Throughout the 1920s and 1930s Germany created a fortified base in East Prussia with fully armed divisions behind a fortified line of lakes and forests called *Wald und See-Sperre*. This East Prussian base was ostensibly to guard against Soviet Russia but it was also aimed at Poland, forcing the Poles at great national expense to build the only true line of fortifications following the River Biebrza on the East Prussian frontier from the region of Augustów to Modlin near Warsaw.[31]

In 1936 a "Western" plan was put forward by the Polish generals of a special section made up of the senior military leaders, which in time came to be called *Generalny Inspektorat Sił Zbrojnych* (*GISZ*). This organ became the main military planning mind of the Polish army. Yet, until March 1939 the "Western" plan was not worked out in detail as was the "Eastern" plan. The Poles did not have any military plans to face a double attack from the east and the west. Piłsudski viewed such an eventuality as beyond Poland's potential strength to resist, except in an armed demonstration against a new partition of the nation. But this possibility was thought to be farfetched because of the difficult political relations between Hitler and Stalin.[32]

At this point, on March 24, Beck defined the political line at a secret conference of the senior officials of the Ministry of Foreign Affairs. Beck stated that Germany had "lost its calculability" and that a number of new elements had appeared in Poland's politics. He stated:

As far as the basic line of action is concerned, a straight and clear line has been established with the top factors in the State. We defined with precision the limits of our direct interests, and beyond this line we conduct a normal policy and undertake action dealing with it as with normal current work. Below this line comes our Polish non-possumus. This is clear: we will fight. Once the matter is put this way, chaos is overcome by a considerable share of calm, and thinking becomes orderly.

Where is the line? It is our territory, but not only that. The line also involves the non-acceptance by our state, regarding the drastic spot that Danzig imposed on us. And, regardless of what Danzig is worth as an object (in my opinion it may perhaps be worth quite a lot, but this is of no concern at the moment), under the present circumstances it has become a symbol. This means that, if we join that category of eastern states that allow rules to be dictated to them, then I do not know where the matter will end. That is why it is wiser to go forward to meet the enemy than to wait for him at home.[33]

Beck also notified the British that Poland was prepared to fight if Germany should occupy Danzig by military force.[34] On March 24 Szembek informed the German ambassador Moltke that Poland could not accept the idea of a German highway across Polish territory, and that Danzig must remain a Free City. Moltke answered in a resigned tone that he was aware of Poland's position. The ambassador ended the conversation by stating that Hitler would guarantee the Polish border. Szembek replied that Poland never asked this of Germany.[35]

During this time the Poles removed all empty rolling stock from the port of Gdynia. The main Polish frontier communication bridge at Tczew (Dirschau) over the Vistula River had been illuminated and sandbagged, and machine guns had been mounted on the bridge.[36] Hitler reacted in a military directive to the commander-in-chief of the Wehrmacht, General von Brauchitsch, which said in part, ". . . The Führer does not wish to solve the Danzig question by force . . . to drive Poland into the arms of Britain." However, there was the possibility of a change of policy:

For the present the Führer does not intend to solve the Polish question. However, it should now be worked upon. A solution in the near future would have to be based on especially favourable political pre-conditions. In such a case Poland would have to be so beaten down that, during the next few decades, she need not be taken into account as a political factor. In a solution of this kind the Führer envisaged an advanced frontier, extending from the eastern border of East Prussia to the eastern tip of Silesia. The questions of evacuation and resettlement still remain open. The Fuhrer does *not* wish to enter the Ukraine. Possibly a Ukrainian State might be established.[37]

Lipski delivered Beck's reply to the German government on March 26. Poland was ready to work with Germany to create the proper conditions for German rail transit customs and road communication through the Corridor, but extraterritorial highway facilities were not equivalent to extraterritorial passage.[38] Ribbentrop at the outset "excitedly" mentioned that Polish mobilization in Pomerania had made a very bad impression and reminded him of the Czech military mobilization which ended badly for that state. The talks over Danzig terminated in a deadlock.[39]

Beck, on March 29, warned Moltke that Poland and Germany had come to a "turning point" in their relations and the "decision now rested with Berlin." Moltke countered that Hitler had given a preeminence to the policy of reconciliation with Poland: the German proposals on Danzig and the highway and a common eastern policy were "aimed precisely at setting German-Polish relations on a sound and permanent basis" which should be understood by Poland.[40]

The stand of the Poles was strengthened by the successful secret cabinet discussions that were going on in London, culminating in Neville Chamberlain's declaration on March 31 in the House of Commons of a guarantee of Polish independence. This first open commitment marked a reversal of British policy in Eastern Europe which historically was marked by a negative lack of interest and hostility. The commitment was announced on the eve of the Polish foreign minister's planned departure for London.[41]

In the last days of March Hitler gave the order to the *Oberkommando der Wehrmacht* (*OKW*) to revamp and prepare plans for a "military contest" with Poland. On April 3 General Wilhelm Keitel, the chief of *OKW*, assigned the job to Colonel Walter Warlimont, chief of the planning section, to be ready at the end of August.[42] On April 11 Hitler signed the directive for the uniform preparation of war by the *Wehrmacht* for 1939-1940. Part of the army was to safeguard the frontiers of the German Reich and defend against surprise air attacks. The prerequisite of the conflict with Poland was its isolation with "sudden heavy blows." The task of the *Wehrmacht* was to destroy the Polish armed forces in a surprise attack if Poland had not changed her policy towards Germany. Thus, it was essential for the initiation of military preparations "to remove if necessary any threat from this direction forever." The plan "Frontier Security East," *Fall Weiss*, did not necessarily expect the western democracies to come to the aid of Poland during the German attack. The surprise occupation of Danzig could be independent of *Fall Weiss*. The army was expected to be ready to exploit a favorable situation by occupying the Free City from East Prussia.[43] The main German thrust into Poland was to come from the Silesian frontier, driving the shortest distance toward Warsaw. A second thrust from Pomerania and East Prussia would cut off Poland from the Baltic.[44]

During the end of March British espionage made contact in Warsaw with Polish intelligence concerning close cooperation and the exchange of data, especially in radio intelligence. The initiative came from the British Secret Service (Intelligence Service), and not from military intelligence. This was a historical evolution, reversing the trend of British espionage which, since the early 1920s had operated against Polish national interest. British Secret Service operated in Danzig, Warsaw, and Oppeln (Opole). It also used newspaper correspondence from the *Times* and other papers. Polish intelligence did not operate in Britain.[45]

In contrast, since 1921 regular exchanges of information were made by Polish intelligence with the French *Deuxième Bureau,* covering all of Europe. Although there were periods of suspicion between the two allies, contacts were never broken between Paris and Warsaw. Beyond the formal contacts there was also intelligence radio communication between the two capitals.[46]

Thus, in 1939 the British began to work with Polish intelligence and received close cooperation, especially in the field of radio communication. Along with the French they were supplied with regular information bulletins, but the western Allies were not yet informed that Polish intelligence had the secret of the German "Enigma" machine.[47] Czech intelligence stationed in London, following the British example, made contact with the Poles in April by sending a Major Joseph Bartik with the proposition of Colonel Frantisek Moravec, chief of Czech Intelligence, and his mentor Beneš, to start an exchange of information and to put the Czech espionage network in Germany at Poland's disposal. The Czech conditions were the following:

1. Poland was to allow the formation of a Czechoslovak Legion on its territory under the command of Czech officers and under the cover of work battalions.

2. Czechoslovak artillery, air force, armor and other technical specialists were to be accepted into the Polish army, until the rise of large Czech military units.

3. Facilitating Czechoslovak forces in the crossing of the frontier and creating a special center where these newly arrived troops could be concentrated and selected.

4. Permitting the Czechs to set up through Polish diplomatic posts radio stations that would have contact with Czechoslovakia. The Czechs also asked to use Polish terrain for propaganda purposes.

In return the Czechs promised to forward German documents and material in their possession, especially important *Abwehr* intelligence documents from their top Dresden agent. Bartik would also inform Warsaw as to the strength of the German army in Czechoslovakia, particularly in the area on the frontier with Poland, and the Czechs would organize anti-German diversion in Czechoslovakia.[48] Bartik's proposals were reported by Polish intelligence to General Stachiewicz. He rejected points 1 and 2, but agreed conditionally to 3 and 4, that only 300 Czech troops per month could cross the Polish frontier and that they could not remain in Poland, but must be shipped via Gdynia-Danzig to the west. The Poles asked Czech intelligence to use radio contact and activity in Poland with "maximum" discretion, as not to give Hitler any pretext for attack, or to supply the French and English with further appeasement arguments. The Czechs agreed to these conditions.[49]

The return of Beck from London with a bilateral agreement drafted on April 6 was given a cool reception in Berlin where his train stopped on the return trip. The Anglo-Polish Agreement was only made formal on August 25, 1939, by a Treaty of Alliance after many delays. Yet Beck had scored a diplomatic success. London would assist Warsaw; Poland's diplomatic isolation was broken.[50] On the Beck train heading for Warsaw reports were given by Poland's military attaché in Berlin, Antoni Szymański, that German motorized troops were concentrating in Silesia, Moravia, and Pomerania, and that the German army was moving in mass towards the east. Lipski also believed that war was coming. Both Szymański and Lipski accompanied Beck on the train to Frankfurt on the Oder, returning from there to Berlin by plane.[51]

On April 28, 1939, Hitler delivered a major speech at the *Reichstag* making public the German demands for an extraterritorial railway and highway connection with East Prussia and for the final settlement of the Danzig problem. Hitler also noted that because of Polish mobilization a "violent" reversal of Polish policy had taken place. The Polish-British alliance was considered by Hitler to be an infringement of the 1934 German-Polish Non-Aggression Pact, thereby voiding that document.[52]

After Hitler's denunciation of the 1934 pact, the Polish General Staff ordered the Pomeranian army with headquarters in the city of Toruń to prepare for a surprise German seizure of the Free City. A Polish military force made up of one regiment of light cavalry with artillery was stationed in Starograd, approximately nineteen miles from Danzig, to prevent a Danzig *Anschluss* by force.[53] This old Hanseatic port on the Baltic and at the mouth of Poland's major river, the Vistula, had little value as a military object, but as a historic political barometer of the interwar period it was crucial.[54]

The Polish military had already mined the strategic bridge at Tczew, to prevent a German military advance across the Vistula from East Prussia using Danzig territory. If there was to be a race for the Free City, without a war, the Poles could beat the Germans. To counter this Polish advantage, in April and May Germany sent to Danzig military *Wehrmacht* personnel disguised as "tourists" to build anti-aircraft and artillery emplacements. The Vistula River was bridged by the construction of a pontoon bridge on Free City territory, so that troops could bypass the Polish Tczew crossing. A second pontoon bridge was built across the Nogat River connecting East Prussia with Danzig territory near the city of Elbing.[55] The Danzig police were trained as a military force. It was estimated that including the SS, SA and *Hitler Jugend*, the forces numbered 7,000; also, Germans from Poland proper of draft age were receiving military and intelligence training from the *Abwehr* in Danzig.[56] These troops, as well as regular *Wehrmacht* agents from Danzig, were sent into Poland.[57] The armament of the Free City was extensive. Polish intelligence within the Danzig government and Senate estimated in October 1938, that there were over 16,000 rifles, 2,000 pistols and over 500 light and heavy machine guns which were stored secretly within the Free City.[58]

In April 1939 Polish intelligence "West" made one of the last breakdowns of the German military strength in detail, but this time on war footing. The German armed forces from the division level were being prepared for war in the east. The Polish-German border was reinforced and reserve divisions were also brought up to the frontier. The Poles gauged how fast German infantry, armor and other units would move over a given terrain.[59]

The following weeks in May saw a steady increase of German-Polish tensions. Reports from Danzig stated that the German newspapers wrote on the possibility that with the removal of Maxim Litvinov as Soviet Commissar for Foreign Affairs on May 3, a return could be made to the German-Russian spirit of Rapallo.[60]

During the same time, Minister Orłowski reported to Warsaw from Budapest that Hungarian intelligence, which was traditionally very close to the German *Abwehr*, informed him that Soviet-German contacts had been made concerning a new partition of Poland and that this news had reached Budapest. This information was sent to Warsaw by special courier letter. A similar dispatch was received by Ambassador Łukasiewicz in Paris.[61]

In Berlin Polish-German encounters in May were becoming increasingly infrequent except for an unofficial meeting at the birthday celebration of Hans Lammers, chief of the Reich Chancellery, member and executive secretary of the Secret Cabinet Council. Unexpectedly Szymański was invited and seated by Marshal Göring's close confidant, General Karl Bodenschatz, who in the past had given Szymański the first warnings of Hitler's intentions toward the Rhineland, Austria, and the Sudetenland. In private, Bodenschatz told Szymański that in the east, Germany could not be surrounded by Poland. If Hitler came to this conclusion, and evidence indicated that he had, then he would break out and make an alliance with *dem Teufel* (the Devil). Szymanski duly reported this converation to Warsaw; twenty-four hours later the Polish attaché was called to Warsaw to report to Marshal Śmigły-Rydz and General Stachiewicz.[62] Yet, the Polish generals and Beck still did not believe in a totally "pessimistic" view of German-Polish relations. The role of the Kremlin could only create a panic in Warsaw, and drive the Franco-British allies into further inertia. It was also hoped that important Nazi leaders, such as Göring, did not favor a Russo-German alliance, because Poland served as a barrier, protecting Germany from the east.[63]

During the last weeks of May military discussions took place with the French and British in Paris and Warsaw. The Poles expected specific French military support at the outset of a German attack. But French inter-war military doctrine was only defensive, symbolized by the "Maginot Line" trench. General Stachiewicz met with British officers in Warsaw. The Poles understood that at the outbreak of the war the whole of German military might could well be directed against them. Hence, their military tactics were to be of a defensive nature. They expected some action from the British air force and also some military supplies from the British. The Franco-British point of view was that Poland was a lost post: the resistance of Warsaw would give the West more time and Poland's victory would then come out of the successful general war. It was planned that Polish technical armor and air force personnel would be prepared for evacuation, and that the best ships of the Polish navy would be sent out of the Baltic to Britain. The Poles gave the British a detailed secret plan of O. de B. (ordre de bataille).[64] On May 20, in the face of the growing tension in Danzig, an incident took place on the frontier between Poland and the Free City. In the border village of Kalthof (Kaldowo), the Polish customs inspectors were increasingly becoming targets of insults and sabotage in which the official buildings of the customs officials were mobbed. The action was planned beforehand to force the inspectors to leave their posts, which they did, allowing a two-hour "military transport" train to enter Danzig. The inspectors notified the Polish Commissioner General, and an investigation team was sent on May 21. As the team was inspecting the railroad station amid near-riot conditions, a group of individuals attacked the commissariat's automobile. In the struggle that ensued the chauffeur shot to death a Danzig SA man. The Germans propagandized this incident as another example of the mistreatment of Germans by Poland. Such occurrences, but of a milder nature, were common; their purpose was to inflame the already tense situation, which was aggravated by the strong Polish stand of not giving in on the Danzig question.[65]

The Polish border was constantly illegally crossed by armed and unarmed groups, destroying frontier markers, signs and road barriers.[66] During the last months of peace the Polish frontier experienced a steady encroachment of German reconnaissance planes over Polish air space. German field radio stations were also in operation within Poland.[67]

To counteract the growing aggressiveness of Germany, Poland in April-May permitted the formal organization of Czechoslovak forces, Vojenski Skupina, in the Cracow region. At the end of May the Czech general, Lev Prchala, arrived in Poland to head the Czechoslovak Cracow center of liberation in Poland and direct the resistance in occupied Czech territories and in Slovakia. Prchala was chosen because the Warsaw government did not trust the London Liberation Movement headed by Beneš. Prchala, as the new Czech leader, had been an enemy of the Beneš policy of appeasement.

Beyond the formation of the regular legion, over 3,000 Czech soldiers were shipped through Poland to France and Britain. The majority of these soldiers had technical training.[68] Prchala also made an agreement with General Stachiewicz that with the outbreak of the war between Poland and Germany the legion would be formally called into existence by the Polish government. The activities of Prchala were followed with concern by the Beneš group in London, which suspected that a new Czech government with Polish clandestine support was being created.

By various methods Beneš tried to eliminate the Czech general, but his efforts failed. A few weeks before the outbreak of the war General Prchala was recognized by Beneš as the commander of the Czechoslovak Legion. In return, for the sake of unity, Prchala placed himself under the orders of Beneš with Polish consent.[69]

By early summer Colonel Smoleński had sent a new Polish military attaché, Wrzeszczyński, to Moscow to specifically observe German-Soviet contacts. Wrzeszczyński reported that as soon as he arrived he noticed Russian officers disguised as civilian tourists traveling regularly to Germany for military staff talks.

In June the Japanese attaché in Warsaw asked Colonel Smoleński if he could make a last effort as a go-between with the German military, because Japan did not look with favor on the growing German-Soviet contacts. The offer was not accepted.[70] Smoleński received information from Leipzig, one of the most accurate sources, that an attack on Poland would come after the summer harvest.

In Berlin, Szymański was also informed by the Estonian military attaché, Colonel Ludwik Jacobson, that General Franz Halder had ushered him, "probably by mistake," into a major staff map work room. A huge map showed the major military thrusts against Poland. This information was considered accurate because Jacobson was schooled in Poland during the 1920s and had close and friendly relations with Szymański.[71]

By the end of June, Polish intelligence in the field was reporting on a weekly basis the German mobilization directed against Poland. The accuracy of these reports concerning the concentration of German military forces was 70 to 80 percent correctly reconnoitered. The main direction of the attack was to come from Silesia against the Polish "Łódź" army, driving towards Warsaw. A second assault would come from Pomerania, severing the Polish Corridor, with auxiliary attacks from Slovakia, East Prussia, and directly from the west towards the city of Poznań.[72]

General Stachiewicz gave out the order in July to Polish intelligence to contact their counterparts in Paris and London, and also asked that the western Allies send representatives to an important official conference. This crucial meeting in inter-war intelligence history took place from July 25 to 27 in Warsaw. The Poles covened this conference to reveal to the British and the French the secrets of the German code machine. The Polish side was represented by Lieutenant Colonel Gwido Langer and Major Maksymilian Ciężki. Major Bertrand represented France although he himself was not a cryptologist. He was a member of the French intelligence cipher section *section d'examen*, and had a thorough knowledge of the field. The British side was represented by Commander Alistair Denniston and cryptologist Dillwyn Knox. However, the leader of the British team, officially called an "observer," was Colonel Stewart Menzies, the deputy head of the British Secret Intelligence Service. During the conference Colonel Menzies was referred to as an Oxford professor who was not part of the cryptological branch, but cooperated with it. The Allies were surprised and pleased at the achievement of the Polish cryptologists; neither Britain nor France had anything comparable in this field.[73] The Poles also promised to give to the French and British Polish-made replicas of the latest models of the German "Enigma." These models were handed over to French intelligence in August. Mayer writes that from the British point of view:

> . . . I cannot say what was the British services' concept of this deal. However we Poles had reason to consider that by the British side it was also treated as an official act of contact between the intelligence services. Commander Denniston and Mr. Knox were introduced to us (Lt. Col. Langer) by the then Major Bertrand as acknowledged representatives of the British cryptological branch. Thus it was by no means a semi-private intelligence affair but the formal contact between two services.[74]

Major Bertrand received not only the two "Enigma" machines, one for London and one for Paris, but also technical drawings of the Polish special auxiliary *bomba* device, enabling speeding the cryptological calculations. The Poles asked of the French and British that close collaboration be maintained in solving the new difficulties which arose out of the introduction by Germany of two additional drums in the "Enigma" ciphered radiograms. It was from these contacts that the French and British received the workable theories and the machines from the Poles.[75]

Since March British-Polish collaboration had become increasingly close to the point that the British S.I.S. representative in Warsaw, Captain Derbyshire, abandoned "unnecessary espionage" activities in Poland. Mayer adds, ". . . the presence of successive S.I.S. representatives in Warsaw had been formally notified to us." The British intelligence representatives, Captain Ross and until the outbreak of war, Colonel Shelly, "loyally collaborated" with Polish intelligence on matters of mutual interest.[76]

At this stage, the outbreak of war was only a matter of time. The long Polish-German frontier experienced daily illegal crossings, primarily for the purpose of espionage and diversion. The border incidents were in two major categories:

(A) Border crossings that were vandalistic, i.e., destruction of border signs and posts.

(B) Skirmishes in which armed troops and paramilitary forces crossed the frontier and attacked border guard posts, border railway depots, and customs offices, with the loss of life almost daily.[77]

The most serious border crisis took place during late August.[78] The first incident happened in the Jabłonków Pass in the Carpathian Mountains, where German *Wehrmacht* mountain infantry attacked the strategic area from Slovakia before the revocation of orders, which did not arrive on time. A special *Abwehr* group, *Sonder Kommandos* "Brandenburg," made up of thirty people led by a Lieutenant Albrecht Herzner attacked the night of August 25-26 the nearly-empty Polish rail station at the town of Mosty. The station was not guarded by Polish troops, and no casualties ensued. The station master escaped during the attack and warned the Polish forces who were guarding the Jabłonków tunnel. The *Abwehr* unit at the station seized a work shuttle train which arrived at the station. They also arrested workers that showed up to take that morning train. The Germans, upon finding out probably by telephone, that war had not broken out, decided to take the train through the Jabłonków tunnel into German-controlled Slovakia. In the wake of the Mosty station attack, the Polish border guards and army personnel had already destroyed the tracks leading to the tunnel. Thus the train was forced to stop and reverse its direction. As this was taking place a fire fight began between the two forces. The Polish troops under the command of Lieutenants Lichter and Osrodka began to surround the train, forcing the Germans to flee with their wounded into the hills, leaving weapons and equipment. The Poles took no casualties. The Jabłonków tunnel was neither seized nor destroyed. The same day an official apology under a white flag was given to Polish General Józef Kustroń by a *Wehrmacht* captain on behalf of the entire German 7th Division in Slovakia.[79]

The second frontier incident was the Gleiwitz (Gliwice) attack, code-named "Operation Himmler." Following a directive from the Führer, Wilhelm Canaris, head of the *Abwehr*, provided Heinrich Himmler with 150 Polish uniforms, rifles, and side arms. Himmler assigned the operation to the SD chief, Reinhard Heydrich. The incident was organized and rehearsed in the Silesia town of Oppeln (Opole). It was to be an attack on a German radio station located in Gleiwitz. On August 31, Himmler's SS troops dressed as Polish soldiers took the station by "surprise" and broadcasted a statement saying that the city of Gleiwitz was under Polish control. They called in an inflammatory speech in Polish for the population to rise up against Nazi Germany. The SS force departed leaving "casualties," who were concentration camp inmates, recently killed by special injections. These inmates, code-named "Canned Goods," were dressed as Polish soldiers and scattered around the grounds of the radio compound, appearing to have been killed by German police who had supposedly arrived and surprised the intruders. The foreign and German press corps were shown the "evidence" of the attack, and the incident was duly reported to the world.[80]

The events were now developing quickly and it seemed that August was the month for the German attack. Danzig, although of no real diplomatic or military value, was to be the spark. The Free City was continually armed and fortified clandestinely and openly by the German *Wehrmacht*, and Nazi paramilitary units, stationed within the city.[81] The Danzig airfield was extended for the landing of bombers, and German troops had been reported on the airfield.[82]

Polish reconnaissance planes from the Grudziadz military airfield in Pomerania regularly patrolled the Baltic in August. They reported that East Prussia was receiving mass troop reinforcements on the division level by sea. Although Polish planes did not cross into German air space they sent spotter planes from Cracow into Slovakia to observe *Wehrmacht* concentration on the Polish frontier.[83]

The Poles had prepared for a German attack in Danzig. At the mouth of the Vistula on the Bay of Danzig, dominating the port canal and the city is the Westerplatte Peninsula. During the Russo-Polish war of 1920 the Danzig dock workers refused to unload supplies and ammunition that were destined for Poland. This act prompted the League of Nations to allow Poland to construct at Westerplatte a munitions depot and harbor with rail communication, garrisoned by a small contingent of Polish soldiers. The building by Poland of a new port in Gdynia caused the Westerplatte base to lose its significance except as a symbol of Polish military presence in the Free City. The installation was secretly built up by the Poles with fortified machine-gun pillbox emplacements and bomb shelters that strategically covered the small peninsula. The number of Polish defenders was 182 men with adequate underground ammunition supplies.[84]

By August 24, all ships had been moved away from the Westerplatte Peninsula, and all normal traffic had been halted to the Polish base; SA, SS, and *Heimwehr* guarded all railroad depots and highway crossings. From the Danzig press Marian Chodacki, the Polish commissioner general in the Free City, received word that the modern battleship "Schleswig Holstein" would enter the port on the 25th. On the open Baltic before entering the Danzig Harbor the battleship had picked up a special assault

Marinesturmkompanie which disembarked at night. The ship was stationed directly across from the Polish base. The "Schleswig Holstein" remained anchored beyond the official given time of August 25-28.[85]

Polish intelligence in Danzig warned the Westerplatte commander, Major Henryk Sucharski, that the base was not to expect any outside aid when attacked. It was to resist symbolically as a "lost post" for a few hours, and then surrender.[86]

Chodacki orderd that all important documents be sent to Warsaw. His counselor and press attaché Wiesław Arlet, burned by hand all ciphers and secret files. Nothing of importance was found by the Gestapo when they seized the buildings of the commissioner general.[87] The Polish Post Office in Danzig was also prepared to offer resistance. Its staff of fifty-one, including some reserve officers, were secretly armed and were ready to fight.[88]

On August 31, Hitler signed the order for the attack to begin at 4:45 a.m. on September 1, 1939. Orders were also given to seize the Tczew bridge and to start the Danzig operations.[89]

Commissioner Chodacki watched from his window the formation of a police and Gestapo cordon of the commissioners residence. The sounds of broken glass and the forcing of doors were echoed by the 280 mm. guns of the "Schleswig-Holstein" firing on the Westerplatte installations, announcing the end of Versailles Europe.

NOTES

INTRODUCTION

1. Jan Weinstein, *Notatka z rozmowy mojej z generałem Pełczyńskim byłym szefem Oddziału II* ("Notes from Conversation between the Former Chief of Polish Intelligence General Pełczyński and Jan Weinstein"), May 1971 (New York: Piłsudski Institute).

NOTES TO CHAPTER ONE

1. U.S., Department of State, *Documents on German Foreign Policy 1918-1945*, Series D, Vol. I (Washington, D.C.: 1949), No.19. Hereafter cited as *DGFP*.

2. *DGFP*, Series D, Vol. I, pp. 433-434. See also: Marian Zgórniak, "Fall Otto i Kryzys Marcowy 1938 r." ("Fall Otto and the March 1938 Crisis"), *Wojskowy Przegląd Historyczny*, Vol. 71, No.4 (Warsaw: 1974), pp. 137-138. Hitler's policy towards Austria met with little enthusiasm from the German Army and the diplomatic corps; he reached out on the 4th of February with the last great purge before the outbreak of war. See: Gordon A. Craig, *The Politics of the Prussian Army 1860-1945* (Oxford: 1956), pp. 495-496; Harold C. Deutsch, *The Conspiracy Against Hitler* (Minneapolis: 1968), pp. 26-27; and Henryk Batowski, *Dyplomacja niemiecka 1919-1945* ("German Diplomacy 1919-1945") (Katowice: 1971), pp. 50-51.

3. Jan Szembek, *Diariusz i teki Jana Szembeka* ("Diaries and Journals of Jan Szembek") Vol. IV (London: 1972), pp. 13-14. Hereafter cited as Szembek, *Journal IV*. See also: Anna Cienciala, *Poland and the Western Powers, 1938-1939* (Toronto: 1968), pp. 50-51.

4. Beck, in Geneva, found the atmosphere to be negative toward Poland. The Poles, even at this moment, did support the system of the World League, although they observed that this humanitarian body was becoming a house of "words" and could be of little aid to Warsaw. See: Jan Gawroński, *Moja misja w Wiedniu 1932-1938* ("My Vienna Mission 1932-1938") (Warsaw: 1965), pp. 477-478.

5. *DGFP*, Series D. Vol. V, Nos. 28, 29, and 30. See also: Cienciala, *op. cit.*, pp. 38-39. The German Foreign Office was informed from Polish sources as to Beck's position in the Berlin discussions. See: *DGFP*, Series D, Vol. V, No.26; Szembek, *Journal IV*, pp. 13-14; and Józef Lipski, *Diplomat in Berlin 1933-1939*, edited by Wacław Jędrzejewicz (New York: 1968), pp. 324-338. Hereafter cited as Lipski, *Diplomat in Berlin*.

6. *DGFP*, Series D, Vol.V, No. 31.

7. Polish General Staff, The Second Department, Intelligence, *Komunikat Nr. 14: O sytuacji wewnętrznej Niemiec, lipiec-wrzesień 1937, Tajne* ("Communique No.14: The Internal Situation of Germany, July-September 1937, Secret"), unpublished communiqué (London: Sikorski Institute), p. 61. Hereafter cited as *K14*.

8. *K14*, pp. 62-63.

9. *K14*, pp. 14-15. Polish intelligence also observed the National Socialist Organization of the German minority in Poland and in other parts of Europe. See: *K14*, pp. 1-5 and pp. 99-102.

10. See the work by F. W. Winterbotham, *The Ultra Secret* (New York: 1974). Also see: Charles Whiting, *The Spymasters* (New York: 1976).

11. *Interviews with the Chief of Polish Counter-Intelligence, Colonel Stefan Mayer*, January 15, 1976. Hereafter cited as *Mayer Interviews*.

12. Tadeusz Lisicki, unpublished paper on "Enigma" (in author's files), pp. 1-2. Hereafter cited as Lisicki, *Enigma*.

13. *Ibid.*, p. 1.

14. Stefan Mayer, *The Breaking up of the German Ciphering Machine "Enigma" by the Cryptological Section in the 2-nd Department of the Polish Armed Forces' General Staff* (New York: Piłsudski Institute), May 1974, p. 1. Hereafter cited as Mayer, *Enigma*.

15. Interview with one of such students, Professor Zygmunt Butlewski, December 29, 1975. See also: Kisicki, *Enigma*, p. 1.

16. *Ibid.*, p. 2. See the published series in Poland on the "Enigma" by Władysław Kozaczuk in *Stolica*, 1974-1975, Nos. 1409-1440.

17. Mayer, *Enigma*, pp. 1-2.

18. Lisicki, *Enigma*, pp. 4-5.

19. Mayer, *Enigma*, pp. 2-3.

20. Lisicki, *Enigma*, pp. 3-4.

21. Letter of Mr. T. Lisicki to the author, April 28, 1976. Also *Interview with the Last Chief of Polish Intelligence General Józef Smoleński*, January 16, 1976, (in author's files). Hereafter cited as *Smoleński Interview*.

22. *Interview with Jan Leśniak*, January 15, 1976; and *Lesniak Report* (in author's possession), p. 1.

23. *Leśniak Interview*, January 15, 1976. The German "Enigma" cipher machine was adapted by the Imperial Japanese Navy, which in turn lent it to the Foreign Ministry, which again changed some of its operating parts. See: David Kahn, *The Code Breakers* (New York: 1973), p. 21.

24. Szembek, *Journal IV*, pp. 18-21 and 30-32. See also: C.A. Macartney, *October Fifteenth* (Edinburgh, 1961), pp. 209-210; and Maciej Koźmiński, *Polska i Węgry 1938-1939* ("Poland and Hungary 1938-1939") (Wrocław: 1970), pp. 56-58. *Interviews with Adam Ciołkosz*, leading pre-war socialist politician, January 16, 1976. Hereafter cited as *Ciołkosz Interviews*.

25. See the Kurt von Schuschnigg memoirs, *Austrian Requiem* (New York: 1946). See also: Henryk Batowski, *Austria i Sudety 1919-1938* ("Austria and the Sudetenland 1919-1938") (Poznań: 1968), pp. 194-198; and Zgórniak, *op. cit.*, p. 141.

26. *DGFP*, Series D, Vol. I, Nos. 294 and 295. On February 12, 1938 Hitler approved the suggestion by the Chief of the *Wehrmacht*, General Wilhelm Keitel, that "false but credible information should be spread and maneuvers near the border executed, creating the impression that detailed military preparations were being undertaken against Austria," yet neither the German Army nor the Air Force was to conduct any real military armed preparations: *Ibid.*, p. 520. See also: Jurgen Gehl, *Austria, Germany and the Anschluss 1938-1939* (London: 1963), pp. 173-175.

27. Zgórniak, *op. cit.*, pp. 143-144.

28. Ministry for Foreign Affairs, *Polish White Book* (New York: 1940), No. 38.

See also: Bohdan B. Budurowycz, "Poland and Hitler's Offers of Alliance," *The Polish Review*, Vol. III, No. 4 (1958), pp. 16-29; Szembek, *Journal IV*, pp. 41-42.

29. Marian Wojciechowski, *Stosunki polsko-niemieckie 1933-1938* ("Polish-German Relations 1933-1938") (Poznań: 1965), pp. 377-378. See also: Paweł Starzeński, *3 lata z Beckiem* ("Three Years with Beck") (London: 1972), pp. 108-112.

30. Michał Pułaski, *Stosunki dyplomatyczne polski-czechosłowacko-niemieckie 1933-1938* ("Polish-Czechoslovak-German Diplomatic Relations 1933-1938") (Poznań: 1967), p. 176. See also: Cienciala, *op. cit.*, pp. 47-48.

31. Gehl. *op. cit.*, p. 184. See also: Dieter Wagner and Gerhard Tomkowitz, *The Week Hitler Seized Vienna* (New York: 1972).

32. Zgórniak, *op. cit.*, p. 145.

33. In April 1938, the *Floryda* section was changed. Its new name was *Boruta* and its director was a Major Stanisław Kuniczak. Kuniczak was arrested by the Gestapo in July and left Germany for Poland. See: Władysław Kozaczuk, *Bitwa o Tajemnice* ("Stuggle for Secrets") (Warsaw: 1975), pp. 389-403. See the "top secret" reports of *Oddział II* in *Wcielenie Austrii do Rzeszy Niemieckiej, April 1938* ("Annexation of Austria into the German Reich"), unpublished report (London: Sikorski Institute). Hereafter cited as *O II Annexation of Austria*.

34. Hitler, it was reported, was not sure of Italian reaction up to the last minute because he did not have a clear agreement with Mussolini over the *Anschluss* question. See: *O II Annexation of Austria*, p. 3. The German chancellor did not want to lose face over the Austrian issue, especially after the diplomatic corps-army purges in February; former Foreign Minister Constantin von Neurath was against military intervention towards Austria. *Ibid.*, pp. 1-3.

35. *O II Annexation of Austria*. The National Archives of the United States, A Microfilm Publication (NAVSMA), t. 78, Rol. 300. See also: Zgórniak, *op. cit.*, pp. 145-146.

36. Polish intelligence estimated that this police force made up about 18 to 20 percent of all the police in Germany, including East Prussia, out of a total estimated German police force of 90,000 men. *O II Annexation of Austria*, pp. 1-12, and Zgórniak, *op. cit.*, p. 147.

37. *O II Annexation of Austria*, Map 3/11-12/1938.

38. *Ibid.*, pp. 6-7.

39. Schuschnigg, *op. cit.*, p. 44. See also: Batowski, *op. cit.* pp. 211-214.

40. *O II Annexation of Austria*, pp. 7-8.

41. The Austrian police could no longer be relied upon and the Gestapo was already functioning in Vienna. See: Schuschnigg, *op. cit.*, pp. 44 and 51; Gehl, *op. cit.*, pp. 188-189.

42. *O II Annexation of Austria*, pp. 12-14. See also: Zgórniak, *op. cit.*, p.149. Vienna was reached by the first German patrols the night of the 12th-13th. In the reports of Polish intelligence it was observed that the German Army expected no defense from the Austrian side: *O II Annexation of Austria*, p. 21.

43. *O II Annexation of Austria*, p. 25.

44. *Ibid.*, pp. 34-40. See also: Gehl, *op. cit.*, pp. 194-195.

45. *Ibid.*, p. 27. The Austrian Air Force also was taken over by the German *Luftwaffe*.

46. Zgórniak, *op. cit.*, p. 149. The Viennese Jewish community numbered over 200,000. See: *O II Annexation of Austria*, p. 4. Czechoslovak military intelligence

from Vienna viewed the German move into Austria with misgiving. In the Czech report, many Germans were "surprised that the *Anschluss* evolved so quickly and went so smoothly." After this union the Germans were not yet ready to start a war or move against Czechoslovakia for the following reasons: 1) fear of Russia, 2) the military was not totally trained or armed, 3) lack of raw materials: *Documents on Czechoslovak Foreign Policy, 1938* (New York: Piłsudski Institute. Weinstein Collection), Nos. 412858, 412859 and 626. Hereafter cited as *DCFP*.

47. Gawroński, *op. cit.* pp. 536-541; and Szembek, *Journal IV*.

48. Kozaczuk, *op. cit.*, pp. 402-403. Göring informed the Czech representative in Berlin that the Austrian problem was an internal affair, and that the German Army received orders to stop fifteen kilometers from the Czechoslovak frontier. The Czech minister, Vojtiech Mastny, replied that Prague had not mobilized, but had reinforced her frontier defense. See: *DGFP*, Series D, Vol. II, No. 74. On the day of the *Anschluss* a conversation took place in London between Jan Masaryk, the Czech minister to Great Britain, and Edward Halifax. The British Foreign Secretary told Masaryk that he still believed it was possible to talk with Germany, to which Masaryk replied, "Yes, until the time when they will control all of Europe and up to that time you can only talk with arms in your hands." Halifax asked what Czechoslovkia would do if Germany started border provocations directed against Prague. Masaryk replied that, "We shall shoot." *DCFP*, No. 414226-1433.

49. *O II Annexation of Austria*, p. 4. On March 12, the Czech Foreign Ministry appraised the German-Austrian union to its diplomatic posts as a "de facto" historical incident, that was to come about sooner or later. This view was also held by Prague's allies, Yugoslavia and Rumania. To count on the League of Nations and the Western Powers was "not even in the game." See: *DCFP*, Nos. 412669-412670, p. 523.

50. A breakdown of Austrian economic strength was reported: *O II Annexation of Austria*, pp. 46-53.

51. The chestnut phrase was very popular among the diplomats of the period. See: John Lukacs, *The Last European War* (New York: 1976), p. 41. Before Beck's visit to Rome, the German ambassador in Warsaw told Jan Szembek of the Foreign Office that there was complete understanding between Italy and Germany over the Austrian question. See: Szembek, *Journal IV*, pp. 51, 55, and 57; Józef Beck, *Final Report* (New York: 1957), pp. 141-143; and Stanisław Sierpowski, *Stosunki polsko-włoskie 1918-1940* ("Polish-Italian Relations 1918-1940") (Warsaw: 1975), pp. 527-534.

52. *Ibid.*, p. 535. The Germans did everything diplomatically possible to quiet Polish fears in the Free City during the Austrian *Anschluss*. See: Bogdan Dopierała, *Gdańska polityka Józefa Becka* ("The Danzig Politics of Józef Beck") (Poznań: 1967), p. 261. See Hitler's interviews on Polish-German relations during the *Anschluss* in *O II Annexation of Austria*, pp. 35-36.

53. "Interview with the Lithuanian Commander and Chief General, Stasys Rastikis" published in *Zeszyty Historyczne*, Vol. 261, No. 35 (Paris, 1967), pp. 168-173. Hereafter cited as *Rastikis Interview*.

54. *Ibid.*, p. 168. In the first part of March, talks were to take place in Danzig, but the Lithuanian delegation did not arrive at the pre-arranged time: Szembek, *Journal IV*, p. 50.

55. *Ibid.*, pp. 56, 74, 79, and 84. See also: Gawroński, *op. cit.*, pp. 547-549; Starzeński, *op. cit.*, p. 120. Beck stated on the train that he would work with Italy

to improve Hungarian-Rumanian relations and to bring about an improvement of relations in the international Danube Basin: Letter from Roman Dębicki to the author, 7 August 1976.

56. *Ibid.*, pp. 121-122 and Szembek, *Journal IV*, pp. 87-88. Demonstrations against Lithuania took place in other Polish cities, calling on the military to bring about an *Anschluss* style union with Poland: Leon Mitkiewicz, *Wspomnienia kowieńskie 1938-1939* ("Kaunas' Memoirs 1938-1939") (London: 1968), pp. 9-10.

57. Szembek, *Journal IV*, pp. 88-89, and 104-106; *DGFP*, Series D, Vol. V, No. 338.

58. *DGFP*, Series D, Vol. V, No. 340. There was no secret military understanding between Lithuania and the Soviet Union: *DGFP*, Series D, Vol. V, No. 339. See also: *Rastikis Interview*, pp. 167-170.

59. *DGFP*, Series D, Vol. V, No. 320.

60. *DGFP*, Series D, Vol. V, Nos. 323, 324, and 333. Beck explained to the German Ambassador, Hans von Moltke, the details of Warsaw's intentions toward Lithuania. He stated that Lithuanian anti-Polish agents had, on occasion, crossed the border under military protection and that other illegal activities had taken place. When Moltke asked if there was to be an ultimatum, Beck replied in the affirmative, giving a time limit of 48 hours. The Foreign Minister, during the conversation, stressed that there would be no surprises and that Germany would be informed of future developments: *DGFP*, Series D, Vol. V, No. 330. During this period Polish intelligence was not alerted to prepare for a military invasion of Lithuania: Letter of Col. Stefan Mayer, Chief of Polish Counter-Intelligence to the author, April 26, 1976.

61. Mitkiewicz, *op. cit.*, p. 36. See also: Leonas Sabaliunas, *Lithuania in Crisis: Nationalism to Communism 1939-1940* (Bloomington: 1972), pp. 14-15. As early as March 17 the points of the Polish ultimatum were known to the interested parties: *DGFP*, Series D, Vol. V, No. 327. Lithuania tried through Leon Noël, the French Ambassador in Warsaw, to appoint a representative. Warsaw rejected this: Szembek, *Journal IV*, pp. 88-89; Leon Noël, *Agresja niemiecka* ("German Aggression") (Warsaw: 1966), pp. 158-160. Lithuania also ceased its intelligence work directed against Poland after the exchange of diplomatic representatives: *Mayer Interviews*, January 15, 1976.

NOTES TO CHAPTER TWO

1. *DGFP*, Series D, Vol. II, No. 74.

2. *Ibid.*, Nos. 76-78, and 83. The Poles reported these events: Lipski, *Diplomat in Berlin*, pp. 356-357.

3. *DGFP*, Series D, Vol. II, No. 78.

4. Marian Zgórniak, *Wojskowe aspekty kryzysu czechosłowackiego 1938 r.* ("Military Aspects of the 1938 Czechoslovak Crisis") (Cracow: 1966), pp. 84-85. Hereafter cited as Zgórniak, *Czechoslovakia*.

5. *DGFP*, Series D, Vol. II, Nos. 85 and 91.

6. Zgórniak, *Czechoslovakia*, pp. 81-84. In September 1938 the Czechoslovak Air Force numbered 1200 aircraft: *Ibid.*, p. 90.

7. *Ibid.*, p. 85.

8. *Ibid.*, p. 86.

9. Talks between British and Czech intelligence in London took place during the Austrian crisis. See the memoirs of General Frantisek Moravec, *Master of Spies* (New York: 1975), pp. 106-109. See also: *DGFP*, Series D, Vol. II, Nos. 93, 95, 103, and 107; and Michał Pułaski, *op. cit.*, p. 181.

10. *Documents on British Foreign Policy 1919-1939*, Third Series, Vol. I, (London: 1949), No. 120. Hereafter cited as *DBFP*.

11. The formulation of the note to Prague was already taking place in the first days of March: Szembek, *Journal IV*, pp. 58-59 and 62. The Polish note was also shown to the German Ambassador on March 23rd: Stefania Stanisławska, *Wielka i mała polityka Józefa Becka* ("Great and Small Politics of Józef Beck") (Warsaw: 1961), pp. 86-89 and 102.

12. Szembek received this report from Anatol Muhlstein, a counsellor of the Polish Foreign Office living in Paris and a member of the Rothschild family. The information concerning Czechoslovakia was passed to Muhlstein by the Czechoslovak Minister to Paris, Stefan Osusky. Szembek, *Journal IV*, pp. 98-99.

13. Szembek, *Journal IV*, pp. 105-106.

14. See: Marian Chodacki, *Report on Polish-Czechoslovak Relations* (New York: Piłsudski Institute), p. 11.

15. Chodacki, *op. cit.*, p. 18; Paul R. Magocsi, "The Ruthenian Decision to Unite with Czechoslovakia," *Slavic Review*, Vol. 34 (June 1975); Peter G. Stercho, *Diplomacy of Double Morality* (New York: 1971), pp. 1-5. The Carpatho-Ukraine has been known by many different historical names: Ruthenia, Trans-Carpathia, Carpatho-Russia, of which each had a political connotation.

16. *Konsulat RP w Uzhorodzie 1928-1938* ("Polish Consulate in Uzhgorod 1928-1938") (Warsaw: Archiwum Akt Nowych); Jerzy Kozeński, *Czechosłowacja w polskiej 1932-1938* ("Czechoslovakia in Poland's Foreign Policy 1932-1938) (Poznan: 1964), pp. 219-223; Thaddeus Gromada, "Piłsudski and the Slovak Automists," *Slavic Review*, Vol. XXVIII, No. 3 (1969).

17. Moravec, *op. cit.*, p. 94. Czechoslovak-Polish intelligence cooperation started in 1928, with both sides exchanging information on the following topics: Soviet Russia, Germany and Ukrainian problems. However, from 1934 there was growing suspicion of each other. In the fall of 1935 there occurred incidents with the Polish minority in the Czech Teschen territory, for which Prague blamed the Polish Foreign Service and Polish intelligence. See: Kozaczuk, *op. cit.* pp. 238-241.

18. *Mayer Interviews*, January 11, 1976.

19. Kozaczuk, *op. cit.*, pp. 287-288.

20. *Leśniak Interview*. See also: Kozaczuk, *op. cit.*, pp. 288-290. This does not include the information reported by diplomatic consulates and posts.

21. German intelligence did not find out about this source until after September 1939: *Mayer Interviews*, January 15, 1976 and Kozaczuk, *op. cit.*, pp. 270-274. It has been claimed in memoirs and by historians that the majority of Polish intelligence documents were captured by the German *Abwehr*. See: Walter Schellenberg, *The Labyrinth* (New York: 1956); O. Reile, *Geheime Ostfront, Die Deutsche Abwehr in Osten 1921-1945* (Munich: 1963); Leszek Gondek, *Działalność Abwehry na terenie Polski 1933-1939* ("The Work of the German Abwehr In Poland 1933-1939") (Warsaw: 1974),; Kosaczuk, *op. cit.* However, in September 1939 Polish intelligence burned 90 percent of all documents in three stages. Between September 2-6 Col. Mayer gave orders to burn all intelligence documents with over a million cases and names. These papers were burned in the Warsaw

Electric Power Station. Mayer also destroyed nine volumes of his private notes and intelligence documents. After the Polish government crossed the Rumanian frontier on September 17, all intelligence payment books, with lists of the most important agents were destroyed. Cipher machines were also destroyed. Unknown to Polish intelligence, Major Jan Żychoń from Intelligence Center No. 3 at Bydgoszcz gave his material to the Warsaw Military Archives, so that this material would not be lost to history; it was only these archives that fell into German hands: *Mayer Interviews*, January 15, 1976.

22. *Mayer Interviews*, January 11, 1976.

23. Henryk Dominiczak, *Granica polsko-niemiecka 1919-1939* ("The Polish-German Border 1919-1939") (Warsaw: 1975), pp. 206-208. The use of workers for intelligence purposes was quite extensive. Many office papers and the contents of waste paper baskets from Frankfurt, Hamburg and Berlin found their way into the hands of Polish intelligence. Two specific valuable sources of information were the offices in Berlin of the Reich Ministry and the I. G. Farben concern: Kozaczuk, *op. cit.*, p. 290.

24. *Mayer Interviews*, January 12, 1976 and Kozaczuk, *op. cit.*, p. 392.

25. *Mayer Interviews*, January 15, 1976. See also: Wojciech Wrzesiński, *Polski Ruch Narodowy w Niemczech 1922-1939* ("Polish National Movement in Germany 1922-1939") (Poznań: 1970); Andrzej Szafer, *Mniejszość niemiecka w Polsce w służbie V kolumny hitlerowskiej* ("The German Minority in Poland in Service of the German Nazi V Column") (Cracow: 1971), pp. 117-147.

26. Gondek, *op. cit.*, pp. 329-330; *Mayer Interviews*, January 15, 1976.

27. Gondek, *op. cit.*, pp. 244-246 and Kozaczuk, *op. cit.*, p. 290.

28. *Mayer Interviews*, January 15, 1976. In the 1920s and early 1930s there was the celebrated Jerzy Sosnowski affair which did touch government circles in Germany, but this case is outside the scope of this study: *Leśniak Interviews*. Wilhelm Canaris, Chief of the *Abwehr*, had contact through an intermediary in Switzerland with Polish intelligence located in Bern. Later this information was forwarded to the English and French: *Smoleński Interview*.

29. Letter of T. Lisicki to the author, August 24, 1976, London. The German cryptologists could decipher the Polish diplomatic telegrams, but this could not be done in a few hours as it is claimed: Kahn, *op. cit.*, p. 215.

30. Letter of T. Lisicki to the author, September 14, 1976, London.

31. *DGFP*, Series D, Vol. II, No. 133.

32. J.W. Bruegel, *Czechoslovakia Before Munich* (Cambridge: 1973), pp. 205-206; *DGFP*, Series D, Vol. II, No. 135.

33. *DGFP*, Series D, Vol. II, No. 141. Soviet planes were also reported flying over Poland in transit to Czechoslovakia: *DGFP*, Series D, Vol. II, No. 142. As early as April 8, Prague and Moscow asked Rumania for aircraft transit. The Soviets sent to Rumania their Minister to Czechoslovakia, Alexandrovski, promising the establishment of closer diplomatic relations and to quiet Soviet claims to the Bessarabian territory: *DCFP*, Nos. 412, 305-306, and 378.

34. *DCFP*, Nos. 414028, 414029 and 1285. The Czechs even turned to critics of Beck and the Polish opposition, i.e. the Socialists, National Democrats and the Populists. However, in essence the internal national opposition supported the foreign policy of Beck: Janusz Żarnowski, *Polska Partia Socjalistyczna 1935-1939* ("Polish Socialist Party 1935-1939") (Warsaw: 1965), pp. 395-396; *Ciołkosz Interview*; Cienciala, *op. cit.*, pp. 66-70; Szembek, *Journal IV*, pp. 139-140.

35. Juliusz Łukasiewicz, *Diplomat in Paris*, edited by Wacław Jędrzejewicz (New York:1970), pp. 76-77. Hereafter cited as Łukasiewicz, *Diplomat in Paris*. For the Anglo-French talks see: *DBFP*, No. 164.

36. Cienciala, *op. cit.*, p. 72.

37. *DCFP*, Nos. 413034,682 and 413037,682. The British Ambassador in Warsaw offered his services to mediate all disputes between Czechoslovakia and Poland.

38. *DCFP*, Nos. 412188,194 and 138. See also: *DBFP*, Third Series, Vol. I, Nos. 171 and 192. The British were already informed in April by the Moscow Military Attaché that there was considerable doubt because of the purges and military reorganizations "that the Soviet Union is capable of fulfilling its obligations under the pact with Czechoslovakia and France, especially over the Sudeten question." See: *DBFP*, Third Series, Vol. I, No. 148.

39. Szembek, *Journal IV*, pp. 154-157. Germany denied that any troop concentration had taken place in Silesia and Austria, "apart from peacetime maneuvers," although an "interim" plan to invade Czechoslovakia was prepared on May 20. The final directive for Operation "Green" was signed by Hitler on May 30: *DGFP*, Series D, Vol. II, Nos. 173, 175, 177, and 221.

40. Moravec, *op. cit.*, pp. 109-111. Britain made an official protest against German military concentration on the Czech frontiers: *DGFP*, Series D, Vol. II, No. 186.

41. Łukasiewicz, *Diplomat in Paris*, pp. 84-85. *DGFP*, Series D, Vol. II, No. 186.

42. Łukasiewicz, *Diplomat in Paris*, pp. 90-91 and 109. See also: Lewis Namier, *In the Nazi Era* (London: 1952), p. 182.

43. Łukasiewicz, *Diplomat in Paris*, pp. 110-111. There have been divergent historical opinions of Beck's note of May 24 and the Franco-Polish conversations. See: Cienciala, *op. cit.*, pp. 77-78; and Henryk Batowski, *Zdrada Monachijska* ("Munich Betrayal") (Poznań: 1974).

44. Cienciala, *op. cit.*, pp. 82-83. See also: Łukasiewicz, *Diplomat in Paris*, pp. 113-117. Polish-French intelligence cooperation was very close until the Czechoslovak crisis. During that time a suspicious and cool atmosphere resulted, which was not to improve until the first months of 1939: *Leśniak Interviews*. *DGFP*, Series D, Vol. II, No. 255. See also: Lipski, *Diplomat in Berlin*, pp. 367-392.

45. Józef Beck, *op. cit.*, pp. 155-156. See also: Cienciala, *op. cit.*, pp. 89-92.

46. *Ibid.*, p. 93; and *DBFP*, Third Series, Vol. II, No. 612.

47. Cienciala, *op. cit.*, p. 93; and Beck, *op. cit.*, p. 155.

48. Norman H. Baynes, *The Speeches of Adolph Hitler, April 1922- August 1939* (London: 1947), Vol. II, p. 1490. For Czechoslovak, British, and French reaction to Hitler's speech of September 12, 1938, see *DGFP*, Series D, Vol. II, Nos. 464, 466, 468, 470, and 471. Polish intelligence reported that the Nuremberg rally was organized to clearly present German Sudeten demands to the world, and to show that Germany was ready to go to war. The purpose was to convince the Western Powers that it would be useless to come to Czechoslovakia's defense and thus break Prague's will to resist: Polish General Staff, The Second Department, *Sytuacja wewnętrzna Rzeszy Niemieckiej, lipiec-wrzesień 1938* ("Internal Situation in Germany, July-September 1938"), Warsaw, October 1938, Secret (London: Sikorski Institute). Hereafter cited as *O II, Nr. 18.*

49. *DGFP*, Series D, Vol. II, No. 469. See also: John Wheeler-Bennett, *Munich* (New York: 1948), pp. 104-118; Viscount Templewood, *Nine Troubled Years* (London: 1954), pp. 301-318.

50. *DGFP*, Series D, Vol. II, No. 487; *DBFP*, Third Series, Vol. II, No. 895. On September 15, Dr. Beneš already agreed with some members of his government to surrender Czech territory to Germany. *Mnichov v Dokumentech* ("Munich in Documents"), Vol. II (Prague: 1958), No. 151.

51. *DGFP*, Series D, Vol. II, Nos. 501 and 508. Beck's instructions to Polish Diplomatic Posts were sent before the Chamberlain-Hitler Conference at Obersalzburg. Cienciala, *op. cit.*, p. 112; Wojciechowski, *op. cit.*, pp. 443-444.

52. *DGFP*, Series D, Vol. II, No. 523; *DBFP*, Third Series, Vol. II, No. 928. Anglo-French pressure was continuously exerted on Prague: *Ibid.*, No. 979.

53. Piotr Wandycz, *France and Her Eastern Allies 1919-1925* (Minneapolis: 1962), pp. 398-399. See also: Cienciala, *op. cit.*, p. 116.

54. Soviet Union, Foreign Office, *Documents and Materials Relating to the Eve of the Second World War* (New York: 1948), Vol. I, No. 27, pp. 203-204, footnote 2. pp. 203-204. See also: Bohdan B. Budurowycz, *Polish-Soviet Relations 1932-1939* (New York: 1963), pp. 114-126. Beneš in his memoirs wrote that he could not accept Soviet aid alone, without French and British participation. He did not want his country to become another Spain. Eduard Beneš, *Mnichovske Dny* ("Munich Days") (London: 1958), p. 93; Edward Taborsky, "The Triumph and Disaster of Eduard Beneš," *Foreign Affairs*, Vol. XXXVI, No. 4 (July 1958), pp. 669-684.

55. Henry L. Roberts, *The Diplomacy of Colonel Beck*, edited by G. Craig and F. Gilbert (Princeton: 1953), pp. 587-588.

56. Beck, *op. cit.*, pp. 156-157; *DBFP*, Third Series, Vol. I, No. 1; Roberts, *op. cit.*, p. 598. See also the report of the United States Ambassador to Poland, and his analysis of Polish policy in Anthony J. Drexel-Biddle, Jr., *Poland and the Coming of the Second World War*, edited by Philip V. Cannistraro, Edward D. Wynot, Jr., and Theodore P. Kovaleff (Columbus: 1976), pp. 208-227. Hereafter cited as *Biddle Papers*.

57. Mayer, *Enigma*, p. 3; Lisicki, *Enigma*, p. 7. It was only in France and Britain that this new system was broken in the early part of 1940, but the code's foundation, thanks to the Polish codebreakers, was already in the hands of the Allies.

58. The SD ciphers were read by Polish intelligence until August 1939. The above information was taken from the typescript reminiscences of a major participant: Marian Rejewski, *Wspomnienia o mej pracy w Biurze Szyfrów Oddziału II w latach 1930-1945* ("Memoirs of My Work in the Cipher Bureau in Polish Intelligence in Years 1930-1945"), unpublished memoirs (Warsaw: Military Historical Institute).

59. *Mayer Interviews*, January 15, 1976 and Mayer, *Enigma*, p. 3. See also: Lisicki, *Enigma*, p. 7.

60. Lipski, *Diplomat in Berlin*, pp. 408-412; Wojciechowski, *op. cit.*, pp. 452-462; *DGFP*, Series D, Vol. II, No. 540.

61. *DGFP*, Series D, Vol. II, No. 553; *DBFP*, Third Series, Vol. III, No. 20.

62. For the Polish-Czech diplomatic correspondence see: Lewis Namier, *Europe in Decay* (London: 1950), pp. 285-307. It also "should be noted that Polish press and organs of public opinion have unmistakably worsened" toward Germany during this period: *DGFP*, Series D, Vol. V, No. 53.

63. Namier, *op. cit.*, pp. 285-288; Łukasiewicz, *Diplomat in Paris*, pp. 132-133.

64. *DBFP*, Third Series, Vol. III, No. 20.

65. Łukasiewicz, *Diplomat in Paris*, pp. 135-136.

66. Great Britain, *Survey of International Affairs 1938*, Vo. III, eds. R.G.D. Laffan and others (London: 1953), p. 49; Edward Raczyński, *In Allied London* (London: 1963), p. 8.

67. *New York Times*, September 21, 1938, pp. 1 and 4. Trans-Olza is the Polish name for the Czech area of Teschen. See also: Cienciala, *op. cit.*, p. 122.

68. *DGFP*, Series D, Vol. II, No. 559 and 561.

69. *DGFP*, Series D, Vol. II, No. 562 and *DBFP*, Third Series, Vol. II, No. 1033.

70. Wheeler-Bennett, *op. cit.*, pp. 128-138; Templewood, *op. cit.*, pp. 311-312. *DGFP*, Series D, Vol. II, Nos. 562, 572-574.

71. *DBFP*, Third Series, Vol. II, No. 1024 and Vol. III, Nos. 34 and 45. *DGFP*, Series D, Vol. II, No. 582.

72. *DGFP*, Series D, Vol. II, No. 582. See also: Budurowycz, *op. cit.*, pp. 122-123.

73. *DGFP*, Series D, Vol. II, No. 621. See also: Budurowycz, *op. cit.*, pp. 124-125.

74. Beck, *op. cit.*, pp. 156-158.

75. Cienciala, *op. cit.*, p. 125.

76. Beneš, *op. cit.*, pp. 90-94.

77. Bogusław Kożusznik, *The Problem of Cieszyn Silesia: Facts and Documents* (London: 1943), pp. 46-47. See also: Namier, *op. cit.*, pp. 289-290.

78. *Ibid.*, pp. 290-293.

79. Namier, *op. cit.*, pp. 296-297; *DBFP*, Third Series, Vol. III, No. 55. Papée also received instructions from Beck that if Czechoslovakia would militarily resist, the Polish minister would retreat with the Czech Army and government into Slovakia. See: Kazimierz Papée, "Kartki z pamiętnika" ("Cards from Memoirs") *Wiadomości*, No. 834 (London: 1962).

80. Great Britain, *Survey of International Affairs*, p. 60.

81. James E. McSherry, *Stalin, Hitler, and Europe 1933-1939* (New York: 1968), pp. 58-74.

82. *DGFP*, Series D, Vol. II, Nos. 591-593 and 602-603.

83. *DGFP*, Series D, Vol. II, No. 606.

84. *DBFP*, Third Series, Vol. II, Nos. 1158 and 1231; *DGFP*, Series D, Vol. II, Nos. 603, 610, 614, 618, and 619.

85. *DBFP*, Third Series, Vol. II, No. 1158.

86. Martin Gilbert and Richard Gott, *The Appeasers* (Boston: 1963), p. 165. See also: *DGFP*, Series D, Vol. II, Nos. 605, 607, 618, 619, 634 and 635; *DBFP*, Third Series, Vol. II, Nos. 1111, 1115, and 1121. For the Polish view of the Hitler-Wilson talks see: Lipski, *Diplomat in Berlin*, pp. 422-428.

87. Namier, *op. cit.*, pp. 291-292.

88. *DGFP*, Series D, Vol. II, Nos. 639 and 644.

89. Lipski, *Diplomat in Berlin*, pp. 407-412.

90. *DGFP*, Series D, Vol. II, No. 652; Appendix III, Doc. 112. See also report of German Ambassador at Warsaw, Moltke on the economic importance of Bohumin and the Karvina area to Poland, dated on the 24th of September: *DGFP*, Series D, Vol. II, No. 588.

91. Lipski, *Diplomat in Berlin*, pp. 406-407; Cienciala, *op. cit.*, p. 137.

92. Dębicki, *op. cit.*, pp. 128-129.

93. Namier, *op. cit.*, pp. 296-297.

94. Beck, *op. cit.*, p. 160.

95. Wheeler-Bennett, *op. cit.*, pp. 173-182; Namier, *op. cit.*, pp. 294-300; Great Britain, *Survey of International Affairs*, p. 62.

96. Namier, *op. cit.*, pp. 294-296; *DBFP*, Third Series, Vol. III, No. 101.

97. Namier, *op. cit.*, pp. 294-296.

98. Protest against the *PAT* report by Czech Foreign Minister, Dr. Krofta, in: Namier, *op. cit.*, pp. 300-301.

99. *Polish Press Agency, PAT* (Warsaw), September 30, 1938, p. 1.

100. Cienciala, *op. cit.*, pp. 136-137. See appended map showing the Bohumin Junction to be ceded to Germany.

101. *DBFP*, Third Series, Vol. III, No. 66. See also: Wojciechowski, *op. cit.*, pp. 484-489.

102. Great Britain, *Survey of International Affairs, op. cit.*, pp. 62-64. Namier, *op. cit.*, pp. 297-300.

103. The Czechs were already "confidentially informed" of the contents of the Polish note, when it was handed to Dr. Krofta. The Czech Foreign Minister "made no reference" to the note itself. He stated he would only take cognizance of it and that he would discuss it at the Cabinet meeting. Namier, *op. cit.*, pp. 300-301. Prague also received Polish military maps from the Polish Ministry of Foreign Affairs showing maximum and minimum Polish territorial demands. *Interview on January 14, 1976 with Lieutenant Colonel Kazimierz Skrzywań*, who at the time of the Czech crisis served on the General Staff. Hereafter cited as *Skrzywań Interview* (in author's file).

104. *DGFP*, Series D, Vol. II, Nos. 54 and 55; *DBFP*, Third Series, Vol. III, No.

105. *DGFP*, Series D, Vol. IV, Nos. 6 and 7; *DBFP*, Third Series, Vol. III, No. 92. Foreign Minister Krofta also asked for "pressure" upon Poland by Germany, so that Polish military action did not go counter to the spirit of the Munich Agreement: *DGFP*, Series D, Vol. IV, No. 5; Great Britain; *Survey of International Affairs*, pp. 63-65.

106. Leon Noël, *op. cit.*, pp. 162-199.

107. *New York Times*, October 2, 1938, p. 2. Beck, *op. cit.*, p. 162. The Polish Ambassador to London, Count Edward Raczyński, feared that Polish actions would trap Poland into fighting on the German side; he planned to resign if this came about: Edward Raczyński, *In Allied London* (London: 1962), p. 8. He was assured by telephone from Warsaw that his fears were not warranted: Letter from Ambassador Raczyński to the author, April 9, 1976.

108. Prague asked on October 1 for a delay from 1130 hours to 1300 hours, accepting at the same time in principle the Polish note. Beck consented to the time extension. The ultimatum was accepted by the Czechoslovak government at 1250 hours.

109. Namier, *op. cit.*, pp. 301-302; Wojciechowski, *op. cit.*, p. 485.

110. Cienciala, *op. cit.*, pp. 139-140. In Berlin Ribbentrop telephoned Lipski that Polish and Hungarian interests were being looked after by Germany: Lipski, *Diplomat in Berlin*, pp. 433-435.

111. Polish General Staff, The Second Department, Intelligence, *Akcja Sudecka* ("The Sudeten Action"), Warsaw, February 1939, Top Secret; unpublished communiqué (London, Sikorski Institute), p. 1. Hereafter cited as *Sudeten Action*.

112. *Sudeten Action*, p. 2.

113. *Ibid.*, pp. 2-3. It was difficult for Poles to differentiate which units were being mobilized for the purpose of normal summer exercises, and which for war. *Ibid.*, p. 9. The average German soldier was not informed that he would participate in any military action directed against Czechoslovakia. *Ibid.*, pp. 46-48.

114. See the "top secret" reports of the Second Department, Intelligence, *Niemcy w 1938 roku* ("Germany in 1938"), January 1939, Nr. 23, unpublished lecture (London: Sikorski Institute). Hereafter cited as *O II Germany 1938*.

115. *Sudeten Action*, pp. 3-4. Hitler claimed in a speech to the *Reichstag* on January 30, 1939, that he mobilized 96 divisions against Czechoslovakia: *Ibid.*, p. 3A. Zgórniak, *Czechoslovakia*, pp. 44-45.

116. *Sudeten Action*, p. 5. The morale of German society and of the Army towards Hitler's military preparations against Czechoslovakia was "negative" and generally "anti-war" even though Berlin propagandized the Sudeten question extensively. "The people feared a worse defeat than in 1918." *Ibid.*, pp. 5 and 48-53. Polish General Staff, The Second Department, Intelligence, *Sytuacja wewnętrzna Rzeszy Niemieckiej* ("The Internal Situation of the German Reich"); Communique No. 18, July-September, 1938, pp. 58-60. Hereafter cited as *Germany Nr. 18. O II Germany 1938*, pp. 14-15.

117. Polish intelligence *(Oddział II)* diversionary activity began under the direction of Tomasz W. Drymmer and Major Ankerstein, who organized anti-Czech diversion and sabotage in the Teschen area. The code name of this organization was "K. 7." Its aim was propaganda and military action. The total number of this group was approximately 120 agents. See: Maria Turlejska, *Rok przed klęską* ("The Year Before the Defeat") (Warsaw: 1962), pp. 101-103; Roman Heck, *Historia Czechosłowacji* ("History of Czechoslovakia") (Wrocław: 1969), pp. 365-366. Also a letter from Professor Jędrzejewicz to the author, April 11, 1970 (in the author's files).

118. *Samodzielna Grupa Operacyjna Śląsk: Sprawozdanie z Działania Grupy, 1938* ("Independent Operational Group Silesia: Account of Action, 1938") unpublished typescript (New York: Piłsudski Institute of America). Hereafter cited as *S.G.O. Śląsk*.

119. At the time of receiving orders, General Bortnowski was in Eastern Poland (Polesie) inspecting fortifications: *Lecture given by General Władysław Bortnowski* in Offlag 7-A, Murnau, June 1943; unpublished typescript (New York: Piłsudski Institute), p. 3. Hereafter cited as Bortnowski, *Lecture of 1943*.

120. Bortnowski, *Lecture of 1943*, p. 4.

121. *Ibid.*, p. 6. *S.G.O. Śląsk*, p. 8. Polish Foreign Minister Beck wrote that a plan was worked out by Piłsudski for military operation in 1934, ". . . in the event of the disintegration of Czechoslovakia or her surrender to Germany," but this plan seems to have been lost in 1938: Beck, *op. cit.*, p. 78; Leon Strzelecki's recollections of the 1934 Silesian war games in "Gry wojenne Marszałka Piłsudskiego" ("Marshal Piłsudski's War Games"), *Niepodległość*, Vol. VII (1962), pp. 257-268.

122. *S.G.O. Śląsk*, p. 1.

123. *S.G.O. Śląsk*, pp. 2-5.

124. *S.G.O. Śląsk*, pp. 4-5.

125. *S.G.O. Śląsk*, pp. 8-9.

126. *S.G.O. Śląsk*, pp. 9-10 and *Skrzywań Interview*.

127. *S.G.O. Śląsk*, p. 10.

128. *S.G.O. Śląsk*, p. 11.

129. *S.G.O. Śląsk*, p. 12.

130. *S.G.O. Śląsk*, p. 185; Turlejska, *op. cit.*, pp. 101-104.

131. Beck, *op. cit.*, pp. 160-162.

132. *Samodzielna Grupa Operacyjna Śląsk, Dziennik Urzędowy* ("Official Daily Report") (New York: Piłsudski Institute), October 17, 1938, p. 36. Hereafter cited as *D.U. Śląsk.*

133. *D.U. Śląsk*, p. 36; *New York Times*, October 1, 1938, p. 1. On October 2, 1938, on page 32, the *New York Times* stated that a massive military force of nearly 200,000 troops was ready to occupy Teschen. The total of Polish S.G.O. *Śląsk* forces was approximately 35,000 troops.

134. *New York Times*, October 3, 1938, p. 1. For a recent work on the Teschen problem published in Czechoslovakia see: O. Kana and R. Pavelka, *Tesinsko 1918-1939* ("Teschen 1918-1939") (Ostrava: 1970).

135. *D.U. Śląsk*, p. 37.

136. *S.G.O. Śląsk*, pp. 187-189.

137. Information taken from insert No. 4, *S.G.O. Śląsk.*

138. The restrictions on the sale of alcohol were revoked on the 8th of October: *D.U. Śląsk*, p. 6; Great Britain, *Survey of International Affairs, op. cit.*, p. 65.

139. *D.U. Śląsk*, p. 43.

140. *D.U. Śląsk*, p. 14.

141. *D.U. Śląsk*, p. 47.

142. Bortnowski, *Lecture of 1943*, p. 5.

143. Bortnowski, *Lecture of 1943*, p. 5.

144. Bortnowski, *Lecture of 1943*, pp. 4-6. Police units occupied Bohumin at 10 o'clock the night of October 8, to help in keeping order. *D.U. Śląsk*, p. 49. Polish intelligence reported SA *Standarte Felderrenbalt* attack troops in "Air Force uniforms" in the Czech Teschen area. *Sudeten Action*, p. 44.

145. *D.U. Śląsk*, p. 48.

146. *Rozkaz Nr. 39* ("Order No. 39") unpublished typescript (New York: Piłsudski Institute).

147. *S.G.O. Śląsk*, pp. 190-192; Beck, *op.cit., pp.* 161-162.

148. *S.G.O. Śląsk*, p. 193.

149. *S.G.O. Śląsk*, pp. 192-193.

150. Dębicki, *op. cit.*, p. 156; *S.G.O. Śląsk*, p. 193.

151. *S.G.O. Śląsk*, p. 194.

152. *S.G.O. Śląsk*, pp. 194-195.

153. *S.G.O. Śląsk*, pp. 195-196.

154. *S.G.O. Śląsk*, p. 196.

155. *S.G.O. Śląsk*, p. 197.

156. Raymond L. Buell, *Poland: Key to Europe* (New York: 1939), p. 343.

157. *Rozkaz Szczególny, 9-XII* ("Specific Order, December 9") unpublished typescript, (New York: Pilsudski Institute).

NOTES TO CHAPTER THREE

1. Maciej Koźmiński, *Polska i Wegry przed druga wojna światowa* ("Poland and Hungary Before the Second World War") (Wrocław: 1970), pp. 110-111.

2. Szembek, *Journal IV*, p. 287; C.A. Macartney, *October Fifteenth: A History of Modern Hungary*, Vol. I, (Edinburgh: 1961), pp. 277-278.

3. The dispatch of Csáky was a Hungarian diplomatic initiative to secure

continued collaboration and support from Poland: Minister Leon Orłowski to Ministry of Foreign Affairs, October 2, 1938, *Archiwum Ministerstwa Spraw Zagranicznych* ("Archives of the Ministry of Foreign Affairs") (Warsaw and Hoover
Institution), Nos. 62 and 63. Hereafter cited as *MFA*. Colonel Beck agreed to receive
Count Csáky: *MFA*, No. 72.

4. The Slovak question in Polish-Hungarian politics is covered by Thaddeus V.
Gromada "The Slovaks and the Failure of Beck's 'Third Europe' Scheme," (New
York: Piłsudski Institute: 1970), pp. 59-68.

5. Stefania Stanisławska, *Polska a Monachium* ("Poland and Munich") (Warsaw:
1967), pp. 284-285. The Carpatho-Ukraine area, as many parts of East Central
Europe, go by different nomenclatures which usually have political significance.
Before October 1938 the region was called by the Czech government "Carpathian
Rus." Some students of East Europe use the name Ruthenia. Peter G. Stercho,
op. cit., pp. 2-4.

6. *Sprawy Miedzynarodowe* ("International Affairs") (Warsaw, VII-VIII, July-
August, 1948), pp. 71-73.

7. Lukacs, *op. cit.,* pp. 27-28.

8. At the beginning of September 1938, Hungarian units were based on the
Carpatho-Czechoslovak frontier. The men were called the "Ragged Guard" (*Rangyos
Garda*), after the special "irregular bands" which conducted military operations for
the Hungarian government in the 1920s. The use of these special forces served the
Hungarian government well; it could openly disavow the band activities, "declaring
itself unable to control them," but at the same time these forces were used by the
government to implement Budapest's policy. In 1938 the "Ragged Guard" was
trained, uniformed and led by Hungarian officers: Macartney, *op. cit.,* pp. 237-
238 and 279. During the same period the Hungarian Army Chief of Intelligence,
Colonel Andorka, held conversations in Warsaw. Budapest revealed that Hitler
planned to occupy all of Czechoslovakia up to the Hungarian border: Szembek,
Journal IV, pp. 262-263.

9. Budurowycz, *op. cit.,* p. 128.

10. C.A. Macartney, *Hungary and Her Successors 1919-1937* (London: 1965),
pp. 240-244.

11. *DGFP*, Series D, Vol. IV, Nos. 45, 50 and 112. It is noteworthy that not only
Hungary, Germany and Poland took an active interest in the area, but also Soviet
Russia feared a German-dominated "Piedmont" in the Carpatho-Ukraine. See: Hanna
and Tadeusz Jędruszak, *Ostatnie lata II Rzeczypospolitej* ("Last Years of the Second
Polish Republic") (Warsaw: 1970), pp. 319-320.

12. Polish General Staff, The Second Department, Intelligence, *Sytuacja wewne-
trzna Rzeszy Niemieckiej, październikgrudzień 1938* ("Internal Situation in Germany, October to December 1938") Secret, Nr. 19, January 1939 (London: Sikorski
Institute), p. 22. Hereafter cited as *O II Nr. 19.*

13. *O II Nr. 19,* p. 20.

14. *O II Nr. 19,* p. 21.

15. *O II Nr. 19,* pp. 23-24; Ryszard Torzecki, *Kwestia Ukraińska w polityce III
Rzeszy 1933-1945* ("The Ukrainian Question in the Politics of III Reich 1933-
1945") (Warsaw: 1972), pp. 154-162.

16. *O II Nr. 19,* pp. 15-22. The duties of these research centers also involved
statistical and cartographic studies of Central Europe which were destined for secret

use by the party and state administration. See Leszek A. Kosinski's "Secret German War-Sources for Population Study of East Central Europe and the Soviet Union," *East European Quarterly*, Vol. X, No. 1 (Spring 1976), pp. 21-34.

17. *O II Nr. 19*, pp. 15-22. The Polish government also organized special research centers. One of the most well known institutes dealing with Germany was *Instytut Zachodni* (The Western Institute) located in the city of Poznań.

18. *Mayer Interviews*, January 15, 1976.

19. *O II Nr. 19*, pp. 22 and 24-25.

20. The Ukrainians living in southeastern Poland demonstrated their support for an autonomous Ukrainian state in the Carpatho-Ukraine on October 11, 1938, in the city of Lviv; hundreds of men illegally crossed the Carpathian border to join the newly formed governments, Ukrainian military organizations called the "Carpathian Sitch." See: Stercho, *op. cit.*, pp. 256-257.

21. Koźmiński, *op. cit.*, pp. 118-119.

22. *DGFP*, Series D, Vol. IV, No. 57.

23. *DBFP*, Third Series, Vol. III, Nos. 141, 142, 156, 206 and 232.

24. Leon Orłowski, *Sprawa wspólnej granicy z Wegrami* ("The Problem of a Common Border with Hungary") unpublished typescript (New York: Piłsudski Institute), pp. 70-71. Hereafter cited as *OSW*.

25. *OSW*, p. 74. Polish Foreign Service documents show that counter to Warsaw's wishes Budapest constantly hoped and worked on all diplomatic levels for German-Italian arbitration in order to secure its territorial aspirations. *MFA*, Nos. 80-84, 86, 88 and 89.

26. *DGFP*, Series D, Vol. IV, Nos. 62, 63 and 65.

27. The Hungarians answered through their Warsaw minister, de Hory, that Hungary was too weak a power to take any unilateral action, as did Poland after the Munich Conference. The Regent Horthy also invited the Polish Minister Orłowski in Budapest to have a talk; the Regent tried to explain the weaknesses of Hungarian power and political position vis-à-vis Germany. *OSW*, pp. 72-74.

28. Henryk Batowski, "Rumuńska podróż Becka w październiku 1938 roku" ("Beck's Trip to Rumania in October 1938") *Kwartalnik Historyczny*, LKV, No. 2 (1958), pp. 423-439.

29. *OSW*, pp. 75-76; Cienciala, *op. cit.*, pp. 159-160.

30. The Hungarian Minister in Warsaw informed his government that on October 17, Polish military units were in action in Ruthenia. Koźmiński, *op. cit.*, p. 131.

31. Kozaczuk, *op. cit.*, p. 130. Mieczysław Cieplewicz i Marian Zgórniak, eds., *Przygotowania niemieckie do agresji na Polskę w 1939 r.* ("German Preparations for Aggression on Poland in 1939") (Wrocław: 1969), p. 8. Beck informed his under secretary, Count Szembek, as early as June 1935 that intelligence operations were being directed and financed through the Polish Uzhgorod Consulate. The Polish Foreign Ministry planned to keep the Polish minister in Prague as least involved personally as possible. Szembek, *Journal IV*, p. 312. Likewise, the Polish minister in Budapest and his diplomatic post did not take any direct participation in military operations which were solely conducted by Hungarian and Polish army intelligence departments: Letter of October 3, 1972, from Minister Leon Orłowski to the author (in the author's files).

32. *Account of Polish Military Action in the Carpatho-Ukraine, Fall 1938*, unpublished typescript (in the author's files), pp. 1-2.

33. *Account of Polish Military Action in the Carpatho-Ukraine, Fall 1938*, p. 3. Polish patrols in the Carpatho-Ukraine were made up of complements of six to eight soldiers in civilian clothes. The total strength of the diversionary forces in October 1938 was approximately 53 men: Koźmiński, *op. cit.*, p. 143. The Poles also used intelligence military personnel which took part in diversionary activity in the Teschen (Zaolzie) region of Czechoslovakia in September 1938: Turlejska, *op. cit.*, p. 107.

34. *DGFP*, Series D, Vol. V, Nos. 72 and 82. There were continuous rumors of a coup in the Carpatho-Ukraine led by Ukrainians from Poland and instigated by emissaries from Germany: *MFA*, No. 103. The radio broadcasts were not only anti-Polish, but also anti-Hungarian: *O II Nr. 19*, pp. 22, 23. The same type of tactic was used by Germany in Slovakia. See the study by Henry Delfiner, *Vienna Broadcasts to Slovakia: 1938-1939. A Case Study in Subversion* (New York: 1974).

35. Ribbentrop hoped in this conversation to use Polish interest in the Carpatho-Ukraine as a starting bargaining point in establishing a general Berlin-Warsaw settlement along German-Italian lines: *DGFP*, Series D, Vol. IV, No. 83; Cienciala, *op. cit.* pp. 162-3; Lipski, *Diplomat in Berlin*, pp. 453-8. The Poles received the German proposals with pessimism and foreboding. The relationship between the two countries reached a negative turning point. Szembek, *Journal IV*, pp. 334-335.

36. George F. Kennan, *From Prague After Munich* (Princeton, 1968), p. 64. The Carpatho-Ukrainian government by November 1938 introduced an extensive program of economic collaboration with Berlin. The Voloshyn government turned over all prospecting and exploitation rights to a German company. Stephen D. Kertesz, *Diplomacy in a Whirlpool* (Notre Dame, 1953), p. 43. German-Ukrainian military work battalions were reported to be building roads in the region of Chust. *O II Nr. 19*, p. 24. On October 26, the German Ambassador Count Friedrich von Schulenburg in Moscow first initiated an "attempt to reach a settlement of the questions (political and economic) disturbing German-Soviet relations." See: *DGFP*, Series D, Vol. V, No. 478. See also: *The Report of the Polish Embassy in Washington*, No. 3/5/87, Box 59, Hoover Institution.

37. *MFA*, No. 100. Minister Orłowski referred to the Lubieński mission of October 18, in which Warsaw warned Budapest not to rely on Berlin: *OSW*, pp. 85-86.

38. *MFA*, Nos. 102 and 103. On October 28, the Hungarians formally requested Italian and German arbitration which would have included Poland. But the participation of Poland in the Vienna meeting was rejected officially by Germany.

39. Bethlen told Orłowski that Hungarian public opinion would not accept the Vienna arbitration, and would continue to demand a common border with Poland: *OSW*, p. 87.

40. *DGFP*, Series D, Vol. V, Nos. 93 and 94.

41. Poland received approximately 220 kilometers from Slovakia: Jerzy Koźeński, "Kwestia słowacka w polityce Trzeciej Rzeszy" (The Slovak Question in the Politics of the Third Reich"), *Studia z Dziejów ZSRR i Europy Środkowej*, Vol. X, p. 105.

42. *Germany Nr. 18*; Map 1 in the report. The travel of Polish accredited military attachés was drastically curtailed by Berlin during the Czech crisis. *Ibid.*, pp. 21-23; Władysław Kozaczuk, *Wehrmacht 1933-1939* (Warsaw, 1971), p. 105.

43. Peter Raina, *Stosunki polsko-niemieckie 1937-1939* ("Polish-German Relations 1937-1939") (London, 1975), pp. 137-151.

44. *DGFP*, Series D, Vol. V, Nos. 84, 88, 89, 91, 95, 107 and 127.

45. *O II Nr. 19*, pp. 25-28. It is surprising that so little has been done on the background of the November 7 assassination. *Ibid.*, p. 25.

46. Hungary received the capital of the Carpatho-Ukraine, Uzhhorod, and the important towns of Berehovo and Mukachiv; 610 square miles of territory (21 percent of total Carpatho-Ukrainian area) with a population of 180, 598 out of a total of 725, 357 inhabitants according to the Czech census of 1930. Stercho, *op. cit.*, pp. 279-280.

47. *Ibid.*, p. 280.

48. Stercho, *op. cit.*, p. 281. Hungarian celebrations were described by the Polish press and by major correspondents: Kazimierz Smogorzewski, *Jak sie walił ład wersalski* ("The Fall of the Versaille Order") (text in author's files).

49. C.A. Macartney, *October Fifteenth*, p. 305.

50. The content of this letter was not known to the Polish Minister: Leon Orlowski, *OSW*, p. 97. The Polish historian Koźmiński states that the letter concerned a planned official visit to Hungary: Koźmiński, *op. cit.*, pp. 152-153.

51. *OSW*, p. 97. On November 3, 1938, Hungarian youth and veterans organizations demonstrated in Budapest in front of the German and Italian delegations in favor of a Polish-Hungarian border. The demonstrations had an anti-German tone: *MFA*, No. 109.

52. *MFA*, No. 112.

53. The other participants were Under Secretary of the Foreign Ministry Szembek, Minister M. Arciszewski, Minister to Prague Papee, Director of the Cabinet Lubieński, Vice-Director of the Political Department of the Foreign Ministry Kobylański and Chief of the Press Bureau Skiwski: Szembek, *Journal IV*, pp. 339-341.

54. *Ibid.*, p. 342; Cienciala, *op. cit.*, pp. 165-166.

55. Szembek, *Journal IV*, pp. 242-243. The Poles urged the Hungarians to call for a plebiscite in the Carpatho-Ukraine, hoping that such a plebiscite would be an "open road" for establishing a common border between Poland and Hungary. Nevertheless, Polish diversionary activity was to be continued. *Ibid.*, p. 344.

56. *MFA*, No. 114; *OSW*, p. 97.

57. *DGFP*, Series D, Vol. V, No. 100.

58. *MFA*, No. 118. During this period Budapest had at its disposal 1500 armed men, and it was important for Hungary that their operations in the Carpatho-Ukraine receive support from the north (Poland). Open military aid, however, was rejected by Warsaw. The Poles stated that "they would have no good explanation to the outside world." However, Warsaw let Hungary know that she was willing to continue irregular military action in the Carpatho-Ukraine. See: Stercho, *op. cit.*, pp. 292-293. The Germans too began to intensify their underground activities in the Carpatho-Ukraine: *DGFP*, Series D, Vol. IV, No. 109.

59. *OSW*, pp. 99; Hungary, *Allianz Hitler-Horthy-Mussolini* ("Hitler-Horthy-Mussolini Alliance") (Budapest: 1966), p. 200.

60. Stercho, *op. cit.*, pp. 293-294.

61. *Ibid.*, p. 294. Polish Ambassador to Bucharest, Roger Raczyński had rechecked the attitude of Poland's ally Rumania concerning the Ruthenian problem. Macartney, *op. cit.*, p. 311.

62. Koźmiński, *op. cit.*, p. 154. The indecision of Hungarian Foreign Minister Kánya of Budapest's policy concerning a course of action in the Carpatho-Ukraine was reflected in the reports of Minister Orłowski to Warsaw. *MFA*, Nos. 122 and 124.

63.*DGFP*, Series D, Vol. Iv, No. 118; Galeazzo Ciano, *Ciano's Diary 1937-1938*, translated and edited by Andreas Mayor (London: 1952), p. 193; Stercho, *op. cit.*, pp. 298-299.

64.*DGFP*, Series D, Vol. V, No. 100.

65.*DBFP* Third Series, Vol. III, No. 258.

66.Macartney, *op. cit.*, p. 311.

67.Koźmiński, *op. cit.*, p. 163. For the report of the German Minister see: *DGFP*, Series D, Vol. IV, No. 118.

68.*DGFP*, Series D, Vol.*IV, No. 122. The Hungarian government turned to Rome, interpreting the German notes to the Italians as *desśntéressement* towards Hungary's military occupation of the Carpatho-Ukraine. Budapest planned to occupy the area, and through its military attache in Rome asked for Italian military assistance. Mussolini agreed to send to Budapest 100 Italian airplanes manned by Italian pilots in Hungarian uniforms. But the German Foreign Ministry informed Italy that Germany opposed Hungarian occupation of the Carpatho-Ukraine, and the Italian offer of air support was promptly withdrawn by an embarrassed Italian government. Ciano, *op. cit.*, pp. 196-197; Macartney, *op. cit.*, pp. 132-313; *MFA*, No. 130.

69. As early as November 9, Beck instructed all Polish diplomatic missions abroad that Poland could not be party to any Anti-Comintern Pact. *Documents on Polish-Soviet Relations 1939-1945*, Vol. I (London, 1961), No. 13. Subsequently on November 25, Poland and the Soviet Union would reaffirm the Non Aggression Pact of 1932. *Polish White Book: Official Documents Concerning Polish-German and Polish-Soviet Relations 1933-1939* (New York: 1940), Nos. 160 and 161. It is noteworthy that in the German diplomatic dispatches from Warsaw it was observed that reaffirmation of the Polish-Soviet Pact was intended to counter the rising strength of Germany. *DGFP*, Series D, Vol. V, No. 105.

70. *DGFP*, Series D Vol. V, No. 101; Lipski, *Diplomat in Berlin*, pp. 465-469.

71. The talks took place at the height of Hungarian military preparations aimed at occupying the Carpatho-Ukraine. See: Stercho, *op. cit.*, p. 311. On November 21, 1938, Ribbentrop had sent two representatives from the German Legation in Prague to get first hand information on the situation in the Carpatho-Ukraine. These representatives publicly assured the Carpatho-Ukrainians that "Germany and her Führer have sympathy for the Ukraine." *Ibid.*, pp. 312-314. See also the German report to Ribbentrop: *DGFP*, Series D, Vol. IV, No. 140.

72. *DGFP*, Series D, Vol. IV, No. 132; Stercho, *op. cit.*, p. 308. A copy of the joint German-Italian note was also delivered to the Polish Ministry of Foreign Affairs. See: *DGFP*, Series D, Vol. IV, No. 131.

73. *DGFP*, Series D, Vol. IV, No. 133.

74. *MFA*, No. 134. In his memoirs Orłowski stated that Kánya consciously tried to lead and play off the Axis Powers and finally to receive direct Italian military support in occupying the Carpatho-Ukraine: *OSW*, p. 101.

75. *DGFP*, Series D, Vol. V, No. 252.

76. Szembek, *Journal IV*, pp. 358-359.

77. *DGFP*, Series D, Vol. V, No. 104.

78. *DGFP*, Series D, Vol. IV, No. 139. The Rumanian government, during the visit of King Carol II to Great Britain and Germany which took place from November 15 to 30, let it be known that it also opposed the Hungarian annexation of the Carpatho-Ukraine. *DGFP*, Series D, Vol. V, Nos. 254 and 257; *DBFP*, Third Series, Vol. III, Nos. 262 and 277.

79. *MFA*, No. 135. The German-Italian note was kept from being made public by the Hungarian government. Budapest lifted its economic blockade of the Carpatho-Ukraine although Poland did not, and Hungarian regular and Ragged Guard forces were partially recalled from the Ruthenian frontier. See: Macartney, *op. cit.*, pp. 314-316.

80. *O II Germany 1938*.

81. *O II Germany 1938*, pp. 2-9.

82. *O II Germany 1938*, pp. 11-12.

83. *O II Germany 1938*, pp. 17-18.

84. *O II Germany 1938*, pp. 19-20.

85. Szembek, *Journal IV*, pp. 375-378. The common Polish-Hungarian border concept was also supported by Moscow. Stalin did not want a Ukrainian "Piedmont" directed by Germany. A marked improvement in Polish-Soviet relations culminated on November 27, in a joint confirmation of the Non-Aggression Pact of 1932 and in a trade agreement. Frontier incidents between the two states were down to a minimum. See: Budurowycz, *op. cit.*, pp. 127-134; Cienciala, *op. cit.*, p. 183; *DGFP*, Series D, Vol. V, No. 108. Polish intelligence watched German reaction to the Polish-Soviet Declaration which was extensively covered by the German press as an unpleasant surprise. *O II Nr. 19*, pp. 83-85.

86. Lipski, *Diplomat in Berlin*, pp. 474-481; *DGFP*, Series D, Vol. V, No. 112.

87. *DGFP*, Series D, Vol. V, No. 113. The German ? chargé d'affairs in Prague reported that Warsaw was trying to improve its Czech relations, and that Poland was building fortifications, not only in the newly occupied areas, but also behind the former Polish-Czechoslovak border. See: *DGFP*, Series D, Vol. V, No. 111.

88. Szembek, *Journal IV*, pp. 402 and 407-409. Csáky, the new Hungarian Foreign Minister, inquired if Poland was planning to leave the League of Nations and if Warsaw would inform Hungary: *MFA*, No. 149. See also the report of the American Ambassador concerning the Polish suspicions of the German offers. *Biddle Papers*, pp. 259-274.

89. *O II Nr. 19*, p. 77; Szembek, *Journal IV*, p. 409; *Biddle Papers*, pp. 286-289.

90. Jan Ciałowicz, *Polsko-Francuski sojusz wojskowy 1921-1939* ("The Polish-French Military Alliance 1921-1939") (Warsaw: 1971), pp. 252 and 264. Incidents in the "Free City" were common. Danzig citizens were militarily trained in East Prussia and military stores were magazined in secret in the city. *O II Nr. 19*, pp. 86-103. The Ukrainian nationalist movement was also quite active in the "Free City." Ukrainian students had their own schools and a U.N.O. organization headed by a General Zieliński. *Ibid.*, pp. 93-94.

91. Bogdan Dopierała, *op. cit.*, pp. 315-330. Also by the same author, "Problemy syntezy dziejów polityki morskiej" ("The Synthesis of Maritime Problems of the Second Polish Republic"), *Dzieje Najnowsze*, Vol. VI, No. 3 (Warsaw: 1974), pp. 87-98. See the letter on Polish-Russian relations sent by the Polish Ambassador in Moscow. Wacław Grzybowski to Szembek in, Szembek, *Journal IV*, pp. 378-380.

92. Beck intended to spend the Christmas holidays in Monte Carlo, traveling via Germany. The trip offered an opportunity for an unofficial meeting. *DGFP*, Series D, Vol. V, No. 115.

93. *DGFP*, Series D, Vol. V, No. 119. Hitler implied that Berlin was prepared to recognize Polish interest in the South and the East if Poland became an ally. See: *Polish White Book*, No. 48.

94. *DGFP*, Series D, Vol. V, No. 120.

95. Hungary announced its intention to join the Anti-Comintern Pact on January 11, 1939.

96. *DGFP*, Series D, Vol. V, No. 120 and *Polish White Book*, No. 49.

97. The German Foreign Office did not believe that "any fruitful discussions of certain questions with [Beck] will be . . . possible" yet Ribbentrop should try to "feel out" the attitude of the other Polish leaders. See: Weizsäcker's Memorandum, *DGFP*, Series D, Vol. V, No. 125. The same point of view was held by Beck in his conversation with Szembek: Ribbentrop's trip would not bring about any real "concrete results", Szembek, *Journal IV*, pp. 467-468.

98. Szembek, *Journal IV*, pp. 484-486.

99. *DGFP*, Series D, Vol. V, No. 126; *Polish White Book*, Nos. 50-54. Szembek, *Journal IV*, pp. 479-481.

100. Lukacs, *op. cit.*, pp. 29-30.

101. Cienciala, *op. cit.*, p. 197; *MFA*, Nos. 2 and 5.

102. *DGFP*, Series D, Vol. IV, Nos. 165 and 167; Koźmiński, *op. cit.*; pp. 199-203.

103. *Ibid.*, p. 205.

104. Koźmiński, *op. cit.*, pp. 205-207. Polish intelligence also used the services of the Polish Border Defense Corps, *KOP* and its intelligence section. Letter from a *KOP* guard in the Carpatho-Ukraine in February 1939 to the author, London, February 27, 1976.

105. Stercho, *op. cit.*, pp. 320, 321, and 371. In Danzig and Warsaw Polish-German incidents took place to the embarrassment of the Polish government, which led to a protest by Berlin. *DGFP*, Series D. Vol. V, Nos. 131 and 137.

106. *DGFP*, Series D, Vol. V, No. 305.

107. Sierpowski, *op. cit.*, pp. 557-562; Ciano, *op. cit.*, pp. 33-35; *DGFP*, Series D, Vol. V, No. 136.

108. Relations between Berlin and Warsaw were deteriorating steadily. See Beck-Moltke conversation on German-Polish relations in: *DGFP*, Series D, Vol. V, No. 137. By March 2 Hitler dismissed the Franco-British notes of February 8 concerning the international guarantee of the new boundaries of the Czech state. *DGFP*, Series D, Vol. IV, Nos. 164 and 175.

109. *DGFP*, Series D, Vol. IV, Nos. 183-186, 202, 212, and 228; *DBFP*, Third Series, Vol. IV, No. 239. The Poles succeeded at the beginning of March in receiving from the new Rumanian foreign minister, Grigore Gafencu, the acquiesence of Budapest to Hungarian intervention in Ruthenia.

110. *DGFP*, Series D, Vol. IV, No. 179.

111. *DGFP*, Series D, Vol. VIII, No. 62.

112. *DGFP*, Series D, Vol. IV, No. 198. Macartney, *op. cit.*, pp. 335-336. Hitler sent the Hungarian Minister Dome Sztójay by special plane to Budapest with an urgent message that the breakup of Czechoslovakia was imminent, and that Slovakia would be recognized as independent, but that he had decided not to grant similar recognition to the Carpatho-Ukraine. Thus, Hungary had twenty-four hours to solve the Ruthene problem.

113. The Poles were not informed of these events. Macartney, *op. cit.*, pp. 337-503. The events did receive official Polish support and an offer of its *bons offices* with Rumanian claims towards Ruthenia. Warsaw also would support Hungary militarily if that state was attacked because of her military action in the Carpatho-Ukraine. *MFA*, No. 24, March 15, 1939.

114. Henryk Batowski, *Kryzys dyplomatyczny w Europie: jesień 1938-wiosna 1939* ("Diplomatic Crisis in Europe: Fall 1938- Spring 1939") (Warsaw: 1962),

p. 195. See also: Macartney, *op. cit.*, p. 337. The Czech General Prchala had close contact with the Eastern Section of Polish intelligence: *Report of Colonel Stefan Mayer*, 1940 (in the author's possession). Hereafter cited as *Mayer Report 1940*.

115. *DGFP*, Series D, Vol. IV, No. 210. This telegram was received by Berlin before the Slovak declaration of independence. Stercho, *op. cit.*, p. 374.

116. *DGFP*, Series D, Vol. IV, No. 210.

117. *DGFP*, Series D, Vol. IV, No. 215.

118. *DGFP*, Series D, Vol. VI, Note to Doc. 77. Polish troop movements were reported by the *Abwehr* in a southeasterly direction and the deployment of forces in the area facing the Carpatho-Ukraine. *DGFP*, Series D, Vol. IV, No. 211.

119. Macartney claims that Voloshyn helped the Hungarians by staging a coup on the pretext that the Polish Army was ready to invade the Carpatho-Ukraine. Macartney, *op. cit.*, p. 337. There is no mention of this pretext in Stercho's account, *op. cit.*, p. 375, nor in *DGFP*, Series D, Vol. IV, No. 230.

120. *DGFP*, Series D, Vol. IV, Nos. 235 and 236. It seems the Ruthenians believed that the telegraph communications were broken due to the unstable conditions. They had hoped to receive or draw out German support.

121. *DGFP*, Series D, Vol. IV, No. 227.

122. *DGFP*, Series D, Vol. IV, No. 237.

123. Stercho, *op. cit.*, p. 376. The Voloshyn government tried throughout this short period to come to some direct understanding with Budapest, but all these attempts ended in failure. *DGFP*, Series D, Vol. IV, No. 243.

124. Koźmiński, *op. cit.*, pp. 233-234.

125. The strategic importance of Ruthenia for Poland became obvious during the September 1939 campaign and later, when Poland used the common border with Hungary as a transit area for a sizable portion of her armed forces, i.e., her armored troops, air force and others. More than 100,000 Poles passed through Hungary to continue the struggle in the West. See the study by Kazimierz Stasierski, "Polscy uchodźcy na Węgrzech w latach 1939-1945" ("Polish Refugees in Hungary 1939-1945"), *Przegląd Historyczny*, Vol. III, No. 2 (1961), pp. 247-269.

NOTES TO CHAPTER FOUR

1. *DGFP*, Series D, Vol. VI, No. 40.

2. *DBFP*, Third Series, Vol. IV, p. 269.

3. *Mayer Interviews*, January 11, 1976.

4. Janusz Mirowski (pseudonym), *Fragmenty z dziejów wywiadu polskiego na wschodzie* ("Historical Fragments from Polish Intelligence Activities in the East") (New York: Piłsudski Institute). Hereafter cited as Mirowski, *East*.

5. After March 1939, the KOP was also stationed in the Teschen area and on the Slovakian border, with four centers, and two on the Lithuanian and East Prussia frontiers. *Mayer Interviews*, January 15, 1976.

6. U.S. Department of State, *Dispatch* (strictly confidential), No. 194, October 7, 1939; *Biddle Papers*, pp. 242-245; Wacław Stachiewicz, *Przygotowania wojenne w Polsce* ("Military Preparations in Poland"), unpublished typescript (New York: Piłsudski Institute), pp. 141-148.

7. Soviet intelligence also utilized smuggling as a source of information. Mirowski, *East*, p. 3.

8. *Mayer Interviews*, January 15, 1976.

9. Mirowski, *East*, p. 3.

10. *Mayer Interviews*, January 15, 1976. Colonel Mayer noted that German espionage cases broken in the first part of 1939 rose to the Soviet level which was a constant 300 per year throughout this period.

11. No state had anything comparable directed against the Soviet Union up to this time. Soviet intelligence was not able to set up a similar radio communication network in Poland. *Mayer Interviews*, January 15, 1976; Kozaczuk, *op. cit.*, p. 205.

12. *Mayer Interviews*, January 15, 1976. Polish intelligence also possessed two mobile radio communication centers: a 75-watt and a two-kilowatt station, which in time of war would join the General Staff at its designated command post. *Mayer Report 1940*.

13. *Mayer Report 1940*; *Smoleński Interview*.

14. Letter of Tadeusz Lisicki to the author, April 29, 1976, London (in the author's files).

15. The Poles could also break the Soviet diplomatic code. Letter of Tadeusz Lisicki to the author, September 14, 1976, London (in the author's files).

16. The outbreak of the war and its quick tempo allowed Polish intelligence to give out only four machines: one to the military attaché in Paris, one to London, and two to the General Staff. The rest of the ciphering machines were secretly transported to Rumania and destroyed. The Army Staff machines and one extra intelligence machine were turned over via Bucharest to the Polish forces in the West. *Mayer Report 1940* and *Mayer Interviews*, January 15, 1976.

17. Sergiusz Mikulicz, *Prometeizm w polityce II Rzeczypospolitej* ("The Promethean Movement in the Politics of the Second Polish Republic") (Warsaw: 1971); Wacław Chocianowicz, ed., *W 50-lecie powstania Wyższej Szkoły Wojennej w Warszawie* ("50th Anniversary of the Warsaw General Staff Academy") (London: 1969), pp. 240-243. Hereafter cited as *WSW. Smoleński Interview*.

18. This charge was refuted by Żychoń at a military trial in Britain during the war. Niezbrzycki and one other officer spent a few weeks in jail for defamation of character. See: Kozaczuk, *op. cit.*, pp. 170-271; and *Smoleński Interview*.

19. Lipski, *Diplomat in Berlin*, pp. 499-502.

20. The Gestapo also arrived in Slovakia. See the Jerzy Kozeński article "The Nazi Subjugation of Slovakia, March-September 1939," *Polish Western Affairs*, Vol. XII (Poznań: 1971), pp. 339-340. The Slovak government could only complain by a timid note received by Berlin on March 25.

21. The Anglo-Polish talks were to be kept confidential in regard to Berlin. For the German reports on the Polish - British rapprochement see: *DGFP*, Series D, Vol. V, Nos. 130 and 140.

22. *DGFP*, Series D, Vol. VI, No. 61.

23. *DGFP*, Series D, Vol. VI, No. 61. In the Polish sources Ribbentrop affirmed that Germany would never collaborate with Moscow, and that a Polish-Soviet understanding would inevitably lead to a Bolshevik Poland, and that Germany was resolved to carry out her Eastern program quickly. *Polish White Book*, No. 61.

24. *DGFP*, Series D, Vol. V, pp. 517-530; Mitkiewicz, *op. cit.*, pp. 173-174.

25. Szembek, *Journal IV*, p. 528.

26. Wincenty Iwanowski, *Wysiłek zbrojny narodu polskiego w czasie II wojny światowej* ("The Polish War Effort during World War II") (Warsaw: 1961), Vol. I, pp. 113-118. The Poles also concentrated some 4,000 troops in Gdynia and

NOTES TO CHAPTER FOUR 115

military forces were moved in the vicinity of the Danzig frontier. Berlin noted a "noticeable nervousness" of the Poles, as well as their readiness to forestall a German military occupation of Danzig. *DGFP*, Series D, Vol. VI, No. 90.

27. *Smoleński Interview*.

28. *Polskie Siły Zbrojne: Kampania Wrześniowa 1939* ("Polish Armed Forces in the Second World War: The September Campaign 1939") (London: 1951), Vol. I, Part I, pp. 109-111. Hereafter cited as *PSZ*. See also the article on war planning by General Wacław Stachiewicz in *WSW*, pp. 32-34, and Eugeniusz Kozłowski, *Wojski polskie 1936-1938* ("The Polish Army 1936-1938") (Warsaw: 1974), pp. 313-323.

29. Stanisław Feret, *Polska sztuka wojenna 1918-1939* ("Polish Military Art 1918-1939") (Warsaw: 1972), pp. 84-90. See also: Józef Piłsudski, *Year 1920* (New York: 1972).

30. *PSZ*, pp. 271-272; Iwanowski, *op. cit.*, p. 102.

31. *PSZ*, pp. 111-112 and 358. There was also an established line of fortifications in Silesia, protecting the Katowice industrial are from a surprise attack or a *Putsch*-style seizure of the territory by German forces.

32. Feret, *op. cit.*, p. 98. See also the Polish studies by Restytut W. Staniewicz, "Elementy polskich przygotowań do wojny z Niemcami 1933-1939" ("Elements of Polish Preparedness for War with Germany 1933-1939"), pp. 163-186 and Leszek Moczulski's "Polski plan wojny" ("Polish War Plan"), pp. 187-219 in *Wrzesień 1939* ("September 1939") (Warsaw: 1972).

33. Lipski, *Diplomat in Berlin*, p. 503.

34. *DBFP*, Third Series, Vol. IV, No. 391.

35. Szembek, *Journal IV*, pp. 539-542.

36. *DGFP*, Series D, Vol. VI, No. 85.

37. *DGFP*, Series D, Vol. VI, No. 99.

38. Beck's instruction on the highway were that this was a technical question to be discussed by experts within the limits of Polish sovereignty. Lipski, *Diplomat in Berlin*, pp. 504-507.

39. *DGFP*, Series D, Vol. VI, Nos. 101 and 103; *Polish White Book*, No. 63. the Czechoslovak analogy was probably suggested to Ribbentrop by Ernst Weizsacker, *DGFP*, Series D, Vol. VI, No. 90, marginal note.

40. *DGFP*, Series D, Vol. VI, No. 118 and *Polish White Book*, No. 64.

41. For the background of the British-Polish contacts see: Raczyński, *op. cit.*, pp. 12-15. The initiative guaranteeing Polish independence in the face of German aggression came from the British, after long and delicate spade work by the Poles. Letter of Ambassador Raczyński to the author, London, September 7, 1976.

42. Helmut Greiner, *Die Oberste Wehrmachtführung 1939-1943* (Wiesbaden: 1951), p. 30.

43. *DGFP*, Series D, Vol. VI, No. 185; Bogdan Czarnecki, *Fall Weiss* ("Case White") (Warsaw: 1961), pp. 116-120.

44. *PSZ*, pp. 433-434; Ferret, *op. cit.*, p. 103.

45. During the 1920s British Captain Percy Germains and a Major Keating made up a twenty-eight man intelligence team, which directed its work against Poland since that state was an ally of France. Leszek Gondek, "Antyhitlerowska współpraca Oddziału II Sztabu Głównego WP z wywiadami innych państw" ("Anti-Hitler Polish Intelligence Cooperation with Other Countries") *Przegląd Zachodni*, Vol. XXXI, No. 1 (Poznań: 1975), pp. 69-71 and 85-86.

116   NOTES

46. *Ibid.,* pp. 69-71.

47. *Ibid.,* p. 89.

48. Tadeusz Szumowski, "Legia Czechów i Słowaków" ("Czech and Slovak Legion"), *Kierunki,* No. 20, 1st part (Cracow: 1968). The Czechs also proposed to the Poles the purchase of Skoda Czechoslovak Armaments in October 1938. Due to Polish suspicions and fear of provoking Hitler, the secret talks scheduled for March 10th were postponed until May; four days later Prague was occupied by German troops. Gondek, "Anti-Hitler Polish Intelligence Cooperation," *op. cit.,* pp. 93-95.

49. Jerzy Kupliński, "Z dziejów wychodźstwa czechosłowackiego w Polsce po zaborze Czechosłowacji" ("The Chronicle of Czechoslovak Refugees in 1939 in Poland After the Fall of Czechoslovakia") *Studia z Dziejów ZSRR i Europy Srodkowej,* Vol. X (Wrocław: 1974), pp. 151-152. Many hundreds of Jews, Communists, and anti-Nazi Germans also crossed the Polish frontier and were given aid and papers to travel to England and France. Kupliński, *op. cit.,* pp. 147-148.

50. His Majesty's Stationery Office, *The British War Blue Book* (New York: 1939), Nos. 18 and 19. Hereafter cited as *Blue Book.* The 1939 *Blue Book* does not include the August secret protocol. Szembek, *Journal IV,* p. 769. An important study was done by one of the direct participants, Władysław W. Kulski, in his report "The Anglo-Polish Agreement of August 25, 1939," *The Polish Review,* Vol. XXI, Nos. 1-2 (1976).

51. Starzeński, *op. cit.,* pp. 206-207; Antoni Szymański, *Zły sąsiad* ("Bad Neighbor") (London: 1959), pp. 128-129 and 157.

52. *DGFP,* Series D, Vol. IV, No. 276; *Blue Book,* No. 13. A memorandum was also sent to the British government denouncing the Anglo-German Naval Agreement of June 22, 1935, because of the British policy of "encirclement"; *DGFP,* Series D, Vol. IV, No. 277. It is to be noted that Hitler in his April 28 speech did not attack the communist movement or Soviet Russia.

53. Jerzy Kirchmayer, *Kilka zagadnień polskich 1939-1944* ("A Few Polish Questions 1939-1944") (Warsaw: 1959), pp. 59-60. Iwanowski, *op. cit.,* p. 106.

54. Two studies on the Danzig question have recently been published: Christopher M. Kimmich, *The Free City* (Yale: 1968) and Herbert S. Levine, *Hitler's Free City* (Chicago: 1973).

55. Levine, *op. cit.,* pp. 150-151.

56. Marian Chodacki, *Sprawozdanie Komisarza Generalnego Rzeczypospolitej w Gdańsku do Ministerstwa Spraw Zagranicznych* ("The Report of Gdańsk Commissioner General to the Ministry of Foreign Affairs"), secret, April 26, 1939 (London: Sikorski Institute). Hereafter cited as *KGRP.*

57. Stanisław Mikos, *Działalność Komisariatu Generalnego Rzeczypospolitej Polskiej w wolnym mieście Gdańsku 1920-1939* ("The Activities of the Polish Commissariat-General in Gdańsk 1920-1939") (Warsaw: 1971), p. 354.

58. Mikos, *op. cit.,* p. 355.

59. The Second Department, Intelligence, *Krótki informator o organizacji niemieckich sił zbrojnych* ("A Short Information Guide on the Organization of German Military Strength"), Secret, Warsaw, April 1939, unpublished document (London: Sikorski Institute), No. 160.

60. *KGRP,* May 11, 1939.

61. Leon Orłowski, *Pierwsze wiadomości o nowym rozbiorze Polski* ("First News of the New Partition of Poland") unpublished paper (New York: Piłsudski

NOTES TO CHAPTER FOUR

117

Institute). It seems that the initiative for the first contacts came from the Soviets. Moscow hoped to deflect Hitler's eastern drive from the east to the west. The contacts were made by the respective Soviet-Nazi intelligence departments in Prague, using the former Czech General, Jan Sirowy, as a go-between, since he was in touch with the Soviet intelligence network in Czechoslovakia.

62. Szymański, *op. cit.*, pp. 139-140. Bodenschatz earlier, on May 7, warned the French ambassador in Berlin, Robert Coulondre, that Hitler would come to an understanding with Russia. *The French Yellow Book* (London, 1939), No. 123. See also: Namier, *op. cit.*, pp. 262-263; Jon Kimche, *The Unfought Battle* (London: 1968), pp. 36-40. Śmigły-Rydz was also informed that a German attack was coming by the top Polish Berlin correspondent of *Gazeta Polska*, Kazimierz M. Smogorzewski. Letter to the author, London, April 16, 1974.

63. Szymański, *op. cit.*, pp. 143-144; *Smoleński Interview*.

64. For the Warsaw-Paris-London military talks, May-June, see: Łukasiewicz, *Diplomat in Paris*, pp. 210-222; PSZ, Vol. I, pp. 96-101; *Protocols of the Polish-French General Staff Conferences in Paris 1939* (London: Sikorski Institute, 1958), pp. 1-15; *Protocols of the Polish-British General Staff Conferences in Warsaw, May 1939* (London: Sikorski Institute, 1958), pp. 3-35; PSZ, Vol. I, pp. 101-105; Andrzej Rzepniewski, *Obrona Wybrzeża w 1939 r* ("Defense of the Coast in 1939") (Warsaw: 1970), p. 200.

65. Mikos, *op. cit.*, pp. 364-366. The chauffer's description of the incident was that shots were fired first by the Germans. *Dziennik Polski*, London, August 31, 1976. This adamant Polish position can be explained in terms of previous cases; Warsaw was not going to follow the earlier policies of Prague and others in the face of Nazi demands or agitation.

66. Dominiczak, *op. cit.*, pp. 265-266.

67. Kozaczuk, *op. cit.*, pp. 430-431.

68. Kupliński, *op. cit.*, p. 154.

69. One of the commanders of the Czechoslovak Legion in Poland was Ludvik Svoboda, the future president of Czechoslovakia. Svoboda, after September 17, 1939, led the future nucleus of the modern Czech army of 2,000 men onto Soviet territory. Kupliński, *op. cit.*, p. 154.

70. *Smoleński Interview*.

71. *Smoleński Interview* and Szymański, *op. cit.*, pp. 161-162.

72. Cieplewicz and Zgórniak, *op. cit.*, pp. 11-19 and Kozaczuk, *op. cit.*, pp. 440-441.

73. Stefan Mayer, *Supplement to the Paper of 21.5.1974: The Breaking up of the German Ciphering Machine "Enigma"*, December 1974, unpublished paper (New York: Piłsudski Institute). Hereafter cited as Mayer, *Supplement*. Lisicki, *Enigma*, p. 8; Winterbotham, *op. cit.*, pp. 10-11. Menzies, in actuality, was the head of S.I.S. since Admiral Hugh Sinclair "C" was dying of cancer. Whiting, *op. cit.*, p. 23.

74. Mayer, *Supplement*.

75. Mayer, *Enigma*, p. 4. The Polish cryptologists still had a basic command of the theory of the "Enigma" machine and continued to work on it until the outbreak of the war. The majority of the cryptologists were then sent to France via Rumania. This group was reorganized by French intelligence with the permission of the Polish government with the code name "P.C. Bruno" and continued to work in close cooperation with the Allies. Part of this group reached London in 1942. The British set up their own S.I.S. base in September 1939 at Bletchley Park, near London. The code-ciphering section was called "Ultra": Winterbotham, *op. cit.*,

p. 12. It was only with the help of the Poles that between November 1939 and January 1940 that the new "Enigma" key was finally broken in France and taken to Bletchley. Lisicki, *Enigma*, p. 10.

76. Mayer, *Supplement.*

77. Dominiczak, *op. cit.,* pp. 266-267.

78. The *Fall Weiss* date for the attack on Poland was August 26, but when news reached Berlin a day before that a formal Anglo-Polish treaty was signed, and when Italy announced that she was not ready to enter the war, Hitler hesitated and countermanded his orders for a few days. He hoped that some sort of Anglo-German negotiations would discourage Britain and France from war, especially now that the Molotov-Ribbentrop Pact was signed on August 23-25. A third reason for Hitler's hesitation was that General von Brauchitsch asked for an eight-day delay to complete German mobilization. See: N. von Vorman, *Der Feldzug 1939 in Polen* (Weissenburg: 1958), pp. 44-45.

79. The Jabłonków tunnel was destroyed by Polish sapers the morning of September 1, remaining closed until February 1940: Władysław Steblik, "Niemiecki napad na przełecz Jabłonkówską w nocy z 25 na 26. 8. 1939 r" ("German Attack on Jabłonków Pass the Night of 25-26 August 1939"), *Wojskowy Przegląd Historyczny,* No. 4 (Warsaw: 1965), pp. 287-299. A highly colorful but inaccurate account is found in Ladislas Farago's book, *The Game of the Foxes* (New York: 1971), pp. 208-209.

80. *New York Times,* September 1, 1939; *Nazi Conspiracy and Aggression* (Washington, D.C., 1962): Vol. III, p. 580 and Vol. VI, pp. 390-392; Marian Podkowinski, "Hasło: 'Konserwy" ("Callword: 'Canned Goods"), *Perspektywy,* No. 35 (Warsaw: August 1975).

81. *KGRP,* June 28, July 1 and 20, 1939; *PSZ,* p. 453.

82. *KGRP,* August 3, 1939.

83. *Smoleński Interview* and Kozaczuk, *op. cit.,* p. 431.

84. The most complete study of the Westerplatte Battle is Zbigniew Filsowski's, *Westerplatte* (Warsaw: 1970). All British and neutral shipping had left the port of Danzig that August week.

85. *KGRP,* August 24, 1939; *DGFP,* Series D, Vol. VII, No. 197. The captain of the "Schleswig Holstein" told Carl Burckhardt that he had orders to shell the Westerplatte Peninsula. Carl J. Burckhardt, *Meine Danziger Mission 1937-1939* (Munich: 1970), League of Nations Report. The Polish edition published in Warsaw 270, p. 247. Stanisław Ordon, *Wojna obronna Polski w 1939 roku na wybrzeżu i morzu w świetle prawa międzynarodowego* ("Poland's War of Defense in 1939 on the Coast and at Sea in the Light of International Law") (Wrocław: 1974), pp. 154-160.

86. Westerplatte defense lasted seven days against a force of 3,000 troops, air force, and the battleship "Schleswig Holstein."

87. Marian Chodacki, *Sprawozdania* ("Reports"), unpublished accounts, 1940 and 1941 (New York: Piłsudski Institute).

88. Only after the building was sprayed with petrol and set ablaze did the post office employees surrender. Six were killed in the fighting, six died later in the hospital, four escaped; the rest were shot for not being 'combatants' in uniform: Adam Bartoszewski and Wiesław Gomulski, *Żołnierze w pocztowych mundurach* ("Soldiers in Post Office Uniforms") (Gdańsk: 1969).

89. *DGFP*, Series D, Vol. VII, No. 493. The Tczew bridge was blown up by the Polish Army the same day.

90. Chodacki, *op. cit.*, 1939.

BIBLIOGRAPHY

This bibliography includes works cited in the text and those instrumental in providing background and scope for this work.
These materials were collected from research done primarily at the Sikorski Institute and at the Piłsudski Institute, London; Centralna Biblioteka Wojskowa (Central Military Library) and Archiwum Akt Nowych (Archives of Newer Records), Warsaw. In New York this author consulted the Piłsudski Institute, and in California the archives of the Hoover Institution, Palo Alto. In addition there is an extensive list of taped interviews and letters of the personnel consulted.

I. PRIMARY SOURCES

Unpublished Documents

London
Sikorski Institute

Polish General Staff, The Second Department, Intelligence. *Sytuacja wewnętrzna Rzeszy Niemieckiej, lipiec-wrzesień, 1937.* ("The Internal Situation of the German Reich, July-September, 1937.") Communiqué No. 14, Warsaw, October 1937, Secret.
_____. *Wcielenie Austrii do Rzeszy Niemieckiej.* ("Annexation of Austria into the German Reich.") Warsaw, April 1938, Top Secret.
_____. *Akcja Sudecka.* ("The Sudeten Action.") Warsaw, February 1939, Top Secret.
_____. *Sytuacja wewnętrzna Rzeszy Niemieckiej, lipiec-wrzesień, 1938.* ("The Internal Situation of the German Reich, July-September, 1938.") Communiqué No. 18, Warsaw, October 1938, Secret.
_____. *Sytuacja wewnętrzna Rzeszy Niemieckiej, październik-grudzień, 1938.* ("The Internal Situation of the German Reich.") Communique No. 19, Warsaw, January 1939, Secret.
_____. *Niemcy w 1938 roku.* (Germany in 1938.") Warsaw, January 1939, Top Secret.
_____. *Krótki informator o organizacji sił zbrojnych.* ("A Short Information Guide on the Organization of German Military Strength.") Warsaw, April 1939, Secret.
Chodacki, Marian. *Sprawozdania Komisarza Generalnego Rzeczypospolitej w Gdańsku do Ministerstwa Spraw Zagranicznych.* ("Reports of Gdańsk Commissioner General to the Ministry of Foreign Affairs.") April-August, 1939.

New York
   Piłsudski Institute

Chodacki, Marian. *Sprawozdania*. ("Reports") Paris: 1939, 1940, 1941, 1946, 1948, and 1949.
Jan Weinstein Collection. *Documents on Czechoslovak Foreign Policy: Diplomatic Dispatches, 1938.*
Mayer, Stefan. *The Breaking up of the German Ciphering Machine "Enigma" by the Cryptological Section in the 2-nd Department of the Polish Armed Forces' General Staff.* May 1974.
——————————.*Supplement to the Paper of 21.5.1974: The Breaking up of the German Ciphering Machine "Enigma."* December 1974.
Mirowski, Janusz. *Fragmenty z dziejów wywiadu polskiego na wschodzie.* ("Historical Fragments from Polish Intelligence Activities in the East.")
Orłowski, Leon. *Sprawa wspólnej granicy z Węgrami.* ("The Problem of a Common Border with Hungary.")
——————————. *Ze wspomnień pierwsze wiadomości o nowym rozbiorze Polski.* ("Memoirs: First News of the New Partition of Poland.")
Stachiewicz, Wacław. *Przygotowania wojenne w Polsce.* ("Military Preparations in Poland.")
Samodzielna Grupa Operacyjna Śląsk: Sprawozdanie z Działania Grupy, 1938. ("Indpendent Operational Group Silesia: Account of Action, 1938.")
Odczyt wygłoszony przes Gen. W. Bortnowskiego w Offlag 7-A Murnau w czerwcu 1943. ("Lecture given by General W. Bortnowski in Offlag 7-A, Murnau, June 1943.")
Dziennik Urzędowy przy Dowódcy Samodzielnej Grupy Operacyjnej Śląsk. ("Official Daily Report of Independent Operational Group Silesia.")
Independent Operational Group Silesia. *Rozkaz Nr. 39.* ("Order No. 39.")
——————————. *Rozkaz Szczególny.* ("Specific Order.")
Przegląd Miesięczny i Tablice Statystyczne: wpływ przyłączenia Śląska Zaolziańskiego na koniukturę gospodarczą Polski. ("Monthly Statistical Review: Influence of the Trans-Olza Annexation on Polish Internal Economics.") January-March, 1939.
Obsada Personalna Sztabu Samodzielnej Grupy Operacyjnej Śląsk. ("Military Staff of Independent Operational Group Silesia.")
Weinstein, Jan. *Notatka z rozmowy mojej z generałem Pełczyńskim.* ("Notes from Conversation between General Pełczyński and Jan Weinstein.") May 1971.

Warsaw
  Archiwum Akt Nowych (Archives of Newer Records)

Archiwum Ministerstwa Spraw Zagranicznych, 1937-1939. ("Archives of the /Polish/ Ministry of Foreign Affairs, 1937-1939.")

  Wojskowy Instytut Historyczny (Military Historical Institute)

Rejewski, Marian. *Wspomnienia o mej pracy w biurze szyfrów O. II w latach 1930-1945.* ("Memoirs of my Work in the Cipher Bureau in Polish Intelligence in the Years 1930-1945.")

Washington, D.C.
  Diplomatic Branch, Civil Archives Division

Embassy of the United States of America, Warsaw. *Diplomatic Reports, 1937-1939.* A Microfilm Publication.

Palo Alto
  Hoover Institution
Archives of the Polish Embassy in Washington, D.C.

Orłowski, Leon. *Sprawozdania dyplomatyczne do Ministerstwa Spraw Zagranicznych, Budapest 1933-1940.* ("Diplomatic Reports to the Ministry of Foreign Affairs, Budapest 1933-1940.")
Zawisza Deposit. *Coded Messages Received and Sent by the Polish Legation in Budapest, September 15-August 28, 1939.*

Materials in Author's Possession

Mayer, Stefan. *Sprawozdanie.* ("Report") January, 1940.
Lisicki, Tadeusz, *Unpublished Paper on "Enigma."*
Smogorzewski, Kazimierz. *Rozmowa Kazimierza Smogorzewskiego z Marszałkiem Edwardem Rydzem-Śmigłym.* ("Conversation of Kazimierz Smogorzewski with Marshal Edward Rydz-Śmigły.")
——————. *Jak się walił ład wersalski.* ("The Fall of the Versailles Order.")
Oddział ochotniczy polski na Rusi Podkarpackiej jesienią 1938 roku. Relacja. ("Account of Polish Military Action in the Carpatho-Ukraine, Fall 1938.")

Woytak, Richard A. *Wywiad z pułkownikiem Janem Leśniakiem.* ("Interview with Colonel Jan Leśniak") January 1976.
*Wyniki pracy: dane dotyczące depesz szyfrowych "Enigma" 6.VIII.
1939-21.VI.1940.* ("Summary Data Concerning Deciphered 'Enigma'
Messages, July 6, 1939 - June 21, 1940.")

Taped Interviews

Interview with Professor Zygmunt Butlewski. Poznań, Poland. December
29, 1975.
Interview with Adam Ciołkosz. London, England. January 16, 1976.
Interview with Colonel Jan Leśniak. London, England. January 15, 1976.
Interviews with Colonel Stefan Mayer. London, England. January 11
and 15, 1976.
Interview with Lieutenant Colonel Kazimierz Skrzywań. London, England.
January 14, 1976.
Interview with Kazimierz Smogorzewski. London, England. January
18, 1976.
Interview with General Józef Smoleński. London, England. January
16, 1976.

Letters to the Author

Letter from Minister Roman Dębicki. Arlington, Virginia. August 7,
1976.
Letter from Professor Wacław Jędrzejewicz. New York, New York.
April 11, 1970.
Letters from Mr. Tadeusz Lisicki. London, England. March 9, April
28, June 8, August 28, and September 14, 1976.
Letter from Colonel Stefan Mayer. London, England. April 26, 1976.
Letter from Minister Leon Orłowski. Washington, D.C. October 3, 1972.
Letters from Ambassador Edward Raczyński. London, England. April
9 and September 7, 1976.
Letter from Mr. St. Szmidt. London, England. February 27, 1976.

Published Documents
Great Britain
Documents on British Foreign Policy, 1919-1939. London: H.M. Stat-
ionary Office, 1947-1954. Third Series, Vols. 1-7.
*The British War Blue Book: Documents Concerning German-Polish
Relations and the Outbreak of Hostilities between Great Britain and
Germany on September 3, 1939.* New York: Farrar & Rinehart, 1939.
Survey of International Affairs: Year 1938. Published under the auspices
of the British Institute of International Affairs. London: Oxford
University Press, 1963. Vol. III by R.G.D. Laffan and others.

France
The French Yellow Book: Diplomatic Documents, 1938-1939. London: Hutchinson & Company. Ltd., n.d.

United States
Documents on German Foreign Policy, 1918-1945. Washington, D.C.: Government Printing Office, 1949-1956. Series C, Vol. I; Series D, Vols. I-VII.
Nazi Conspiracy and Aggression. Washington, D.C.: Government Printing Office, 1946.

Germany
Negotiations for the Solution of the Sudeten German Question. White Book, 1938, No. 1.

Soviet Union
Documents and Materials Relating to the Eve of the Second World War. Vol. I: November, 1937-1938. Vol. II: Dirksen Papers, 1938-1939. Moscow: Foreign Languages Publishing House, 1948.
Soviet Peace Efforts on the Eve of World War II, September 1938-August 1939: Documents and Records. Moscow: Novosti Press Agency Publishing House, 1973.

Poland
Ministry of Foreign Affairs. *Official Documents Concerning Polish-German and Polish-Soviet Relations, 1933-1939.* Polish White Book. New York: Roy-Publishers, 1940.
Sikorski Institute. *Documents on Polish-Soviet Relations, 1939-1945.* Vol. I: 1939-1943. London: Heinemann, 1961.
_____. *Protocols of the Polish-French General Staffs Conferences in Paris, May 1939.* London, 1958.
_____. *Protocols of the Polish-British General Staffs Conferences in Warsaw, May 1939.* London, 1958.

Czechoslovakia
Mnichov v Dukumentech. ("Munich in Documents.") 2 Vols. Compiled by Vladimir Sojak. Prague: Statni nakladatelstvi politicke literatury, 1958.

Hungary
Allianz Hitler-Horthy-Mussolini. ("Alliance Hitler-Horthy-Mussolini.") Edited by Magda Adam, Gyula Juhasz, and Lajos Kerekes. Budapest: Akademiai Kiado, 1966.

II SECONDARY SOURCES
Books

Arski, Stefan. *My Pierwsza Brygada.* ("We the First Brigade.") Warsaw: Czytelnik, 1963.

Aster, Sidney. *1939: The Making of the Second World War.* New York: Simon and Schuster, 1973.

Bartoszewski, Adam and Gomulski, Wiesław. *Żołnierze w pocztowych mundurach.* ("Soldiers in Post Office Uniforms.") Gdańsk: Wydawnictwo Morskie, 1969.

Batowski, Henryk. *Agonia pokoju i początek wojny.* ("Agony of Peace and the Beginning of War.") Poznań: Wydawnictwo Poznańskie, 1968.

——————. *Austria i Sudety, 1919-1938.* ("Austria and the Sudetenland, 1919-1938") Poznań: Wydawnictwo Poznańskie, 1968.

——————. *Dyplomacja niemiecka, 1919-1945.* ("German Diplomacy, 1919-1945.") Katowice: Śląski Instytut Naukowy, 1971.

——————. *Kryzys dyplomatyczny w Europie: jesień 1938- wiosna 1939.* ("Diplomatic Crisis in Europe: Fall 1938- Spring 1939.") Warsaw: Wydawnictwo Obrony Narodowej, 1962.

——————. *Zdrada Monachijska.* ("The Munich Betrayal.") Poznań: Wydawnictwo Poznańskie, 1973.

Baynes, Norman H. *The Speeches of Adolf Hitler, April 1922-August 1939* London, 1947.

Beck, Józef. *Final Report.* New York: Robert Speller, 1957.

Beneš, Eduard. *Mnichovske Dny.* ("Munich Days.") Edited by Jan Smutny. London: Ustav Dra Eduarda Benese, 1958.

Bertrand, Gustave. *Enigma ou la Plus Grande Enigme de la Guerre, 1939-1945.* Paris, 1973.

Biddle, A.J. Drexel, Jr. *Poland and the Coming of the Second World War.* Edited by Philip V. Cannistraro, Edward D. Wynot, Jr., and Theodore P. Kovaleff. Columbus, Ohio: Ohio State University, 1976.

Bromke, Adam. *Poland's Politics.* Cambridge, Massachusetts: Harvard University Press, 1967.

Brown, Anthony Cave. *Bodyguard of Lies.* New York: Bantam Books, 1976.

Bruegel, J.W. *Czechoslovakia Before Munich.* Cambridge, Massachusetts: The University Press, 1973.

Budurowycz, Bohdan B. *Polish-Soviet Relations, 1932-1939.* New York: Columbia University Press, 1963.

Burckhardt, Carl J. *Moja misja w Gdańsku, 1937-1939.* ("My Danzig Mission, 1937-1939.") Warsaw: Instytut Wydawniczy PAX, 1970.

Buell, Raymond L. *Poland: Key to Europe.* New York: Alfred A. Knopf, 1939.

Chmelar, Josef. *National Minorities in Central Europe.* Prague: Orbis, 1935.

Chocianowicz, Wacław, ed. *W 50-lecie powstania Wyższej Szkoły Wojennej w Warszawie.* ("50th Anniversary of the Warsaw General Staff Academy.") London: Poets' and Painters' Press, 1969.

Churchill, Winston S. *The Gathering Storm.* Boston: Houghton Mifflin Company, 1948.

Ciałowicz, Jan. *Polsko-francuski sojusz wojskowy, 1921-1939.* ("Polish-French Military Alliance, 1921-1939.") Warsaw: Państwowe Wydawnictwo Naukowe, 1970.

Ciano, Galeazzo. *The Ciano Diaries, 1939-1943.* Edited by Hugh Gibson. New York: Doubleday & Company, Inc., 1946.

Cienciala, Anna. *Poland and the Western Powers, 1938-1939.* Toronto: Toronto University Press, 1968.

Cieplewicz, Mieczysław and Zgórniak, Marian. *Przygotowania niemieckie do agresji na Polskę w 1939 r.* ("German Preparations for Aggression on Poland in 1939.") Wrocław: Polska Akademia Nauk, 1969.

Craig, Gordon A. *The Politics of the Prussian Army, 1640-1945.* New York: Oxford University Press, 1955.

——————. and Gilbert, P., eds. *The Diplomats, 1919-1939.* Princeton, N.J.: Princeton University Press, 1953.

Czarnecki, Bogdan. *Fall Weiss.* Warsaw: Państwowe Wydawnictwo Naukowe, 1961.

Dębicki, Roman. *Foreign Policy of Poland, 1919-1939.* New York: Frederic A. Praeger. 1962.

Delfiner, Henry. *Vienna Broadcasts to Slovakia: 1938-1939, a Case Study in Subversion.* New York: East European Quarterly, 1974.

Deutsch, Harold C. *The Conspiracy Against Hitler in the Twilight War.* Minneapolis: The University of Minnesota Press, 1970.

Dominiczak, Henryk. *Granica polsko-niemiecka, 1919-1939.* ("The Polish-German Frontier, 1919-1939.") Warsaw: MON, 1975.

Dopierała, Bogdan. *Gdańska polityka Józefa Becka.* ("The Gdańsk Politics of Józef Beck.") Poznań: Wydawnictwo Poznańskie, 1967.

Dziewanowski, M.K. *Joseph Piłsudski, 1918-1922.* Stanford: Hoover Institution Press, 1969.

——————. *The Communist Party of Poland.* Cambridge, Massachusetts: Harvard University Press, 1959.

Farago, Ladislas. *The Game of the Foxes.* Toronto: Bantam Books, 1973.

Feret, Stanisław. *Polska sztuka wojenna, 1918-1939.* ("Polish Military Art, 1918-1939.") Warsaw: MON, 1972.

Filipowicz, Tytus. *Sprawa Zaolzia.* ("Trans-Olza Affair.") Evanston, Ill.: Future Press Bureau, 1943.

Fischer, Louis. *The Soviets in World Affairs.* New York: J. Cape and H. Smith, 1930.

Flisowski, Zbigniew. *Westerplatte.* Warsaw: MON, 1971.

Gawroński, Jan. *Moja misja w Wiedniu, 1932-1938.* ("My Vienna Mission, 1932-1938.") Warsaw: Państwowe Wydawnictwo Naukowe, 1965.

Gehl, Jurgen. *Austria, Germany and the Anschluss, 1931-1938.* London, 1963.

Gondek, Leszek. *Działalność Abwehry na terenie Polski, 1933-1939.* ("The Work of the German Abwehr in Poland, 1933-1939.") Warsaw: MON, 1974.

Greiner, Helmut. *Die Oberste Wehrmachtführung, 1939-1943.* Wiesbaden, 1951.

Halecki, Oscar. *The Limits and Divisions of European History.* Notre Dame: University of Notre Dame Press, 1962.

Halifax, Lord. *Fullness of Days.* New York: Dodd, Mead and Co., 1957.

Haskins, Charles and Lord, Robert. *Some Problems of the Peace Conference.* Cambridge, Massachusetts: Harvard University Press, 1920.

Heck, Roman. *Historia Czechosłowacji.* ("History of Czechoslovakia.") Wrocław: Ossolineum, 1969.

Henderson, Sir Nevile. *Failure of a Mission, Berlin: 1937-1939.* New York: Putnam's Sons, 1940.

Heymann, Frederick G. *Poland & Czechoslovakia.* New Jersey: Prentice-Hall, 1966.

House, Edward M. and Seymour, Charles. *What Really Happened at Paris.* New York: Scribner's Sons, 1921.

Iwanowski, Wincenty. *Wysiłek zbrojny narodu polskiego w czasie II wojny wiatowej.* ("The Polish War Effort during World War II.") Volume I. Warsaw: PAX, 1961.

Jędruszczak, Hanna and Tadeusz. *Ostatnie lata II Rzeczypospolitej 1935-1939.* ("Last Years of the Second Republic.") Warsaw: Książka i Wiedza, 1970.

Kahn, David. *The Code-Breakers* New York: Signet, 1973.

Kampania Wrześniowa 1939. ("The September Campaign 1939.") Volume I of *Polskie siły zbrojne w drugiej wojnie światowej.* ("Polish Armed Forces in the Second World War.") London: Sikorski Institute, 1959.

Kana, O., Pavelka, R. *Tesinsko v polsko-ceskoslovenskych vztazich 1918-1939.* ("Teschen in Polish-Czechoslovak Relations 1918-1939.") Ostrava: Profil, 1970.

Kennan, George F. *From Prague After Munich: Diplomatic Papers 1938-1940.* Princeton, N.J.: Princeton University Press, 1968.

Kerner, Robert Joseph. *Czechoslovakia: Twenty Years of Independence.* Berkeley, California: University of California Press, 1940.

Kertesz, Stephen D. *Diplomacy in a Whirpool.* Notre Dame: University of Notre Dame Press, 1953.

Kimche, Jon. *The Unfought Battle.* London: Weidenfeld and Nicolson, 1968.

Kimmich, Christoph. *The Free City.* New Haven: Yale University Press, 1968.

BIBLIOGRAPHY 127

Kirchmayer, Jerzy. *Kilka zagadnień polskich 1939-1944.* ("A Few Polish Questions, 1939-1944.") Warsaw: Książka i Wiedza, 1959.

Komarnicki, Titus. *Rebirth of the Polish Republic.* London: William Heinemann Ltd., 1957.

Kopczyk, Henryk. *Niemiecka działalność wywiadowcza na Pomorzu 1920-1933.* Gdańsk: Wydawnictwo Morskie, 1970.

Korbel, Josef. *Poland Between East and West 1919-1933.* Princeton: Princeton University Press, 1963.

Kozaczuk, Władysław. *Bitwa o tajemnice.* ("Struggle for Secrets.") II Edition - Warsaw: Książka i Wiedza, 1969. III Edition - Warsaw: Książka i Wiedza, 1975.

_____. *Wehrmacht 1933-1939.* Warsaw: MON, 1971.

Kozeński, Jerzy. *Czechosłowacja w polskiej polityce zagranicznej w latach 1932-1938.* ("Czechoslovakia in Polish International Politics, 1932-1938.") Poznań: Instytut Zachodni, 1964.

Kozłowski, Eugeniusz. *Wojsko polskie 1936-1939.* ("Polish Army 1936-1939.") I Edition - Warsaw: MON, 1964. II Edition - Warsaw: MON, 1974.

Kożusznik, Bogusław. *The Problem of Cieszyn Silesia: Facts and Documents.* London: World League of Poles Abroad, 1943.

_____. *Summary of Facts about Cieszyn Silesia.* London: Association of Cieszyn Silesians in Great Britain, 1943.

Koźminski, Maciej. *Polska i Węgry przed drugą wojną światową, październik 1938 - wrzesień 1939.* ("Poland and Hungary before the Second World War.") Wrocław; Polska Adademia Nauk, 1970.

Kuźminski, Tadeusz. *Polska, Francja, Niemcy, 1933-1935.* ("Poland, France, Germany, 1933-1935.") Warsaw: Państwowe Wydawnictwo Naukowe, 1963.

Levine, Herbert S. *Hitler's Free City: A History of the Nazi Party in Danzig, 1935-1939.*Chicago: The University of Chicago Press, 1973.

Lipski, Józef. *Diplomat in Berlin, 1933-1939.* Edited by Wacław Jędrzejewicz. New York: Columbia University Press, 1968.

Lukacs, John A. *The Great Powers & Eastern Europe.* New York: American Book Company, 1953.

_____. *The Last European War, September 1939- December 1941.* New York: Anchor Press, 1976.

Łukasiewicz, Juliusz. *Diplomat in Paris, 1936-1939.* Edited by Wacław Jędrzejewicz. New York: Columbia University Press, 1970.

Łypacewicz, Wacław. *Polish-Czech Relations.* Warsaw: Polish Institute for Collaboration with Foreign Countries, 1936.

Macartney, C.A. *Hungary and Her Successors: The Treaty of Trianon and Its Consequences 1919-1937.* London: Oxford University Press, 1965.

Macartney, C.A. *October Fifteenth: A History of Modern Hungary 1929-1945*. Edinburgh: The University Press, 1961.

Machalski, Tadeusz. *Pod prąd*. ("Against the Current.") London: B. Swiderski, 1964.

Mackiewicz, Stanisław. *Colonel Beck and His Policy*. London: Eyre & Spottiswoode, 1944.

Masaryk, Thomas G. *The Making of a State*. New York: Frederick A. Stokes Company, 1927.

Masterman, J.C. *The Double-Cross System in the War of 1939 to 1945*. New Haven: Yale University Press, 1972.

Mazurowa, Kazimiera. *Europejska polityka Francji 1938-1939*. ("The European Politics of France 1938-1939.") Warsaw: Państwowe Wydawnictwo Naukowe, 1974.

McSherry, James B. *Stalin, Hitler and Europe, 1933-1939*. New York: The World Publishing Company, 1968.

Mikos, Stanisław. *Działalność Komisariatu Generalnego Rzeczypospolitej polskiej w wolnym mieście Gdańsku, 1920-1939*. ("The Activities of the Polish Commissariat General in Gdańsk, 1920-1939.") Warsaw: Państwowe Wydawnictwo Naukowe, 1971.

Mikulicz, Sergiusz. *Prometeizm w polityce II Rzeczypospolitej*. ("The Promethean Movement in the Politics of the Second Polish Republic.")Warsaw: Książka i Wiedza, 1971.

Minney, R.I., ed. *Private Papers of Hore-Belisha*. New York: Doubleday & Co., 1960.

Mitkiewicz, Leon. *Wspomnienia kowieńskie 1938-1939*. ("Kaunas Memoirs 1938-1939.") London: Veritas, 1968.

Moczulski, Leszek. "Polski plan wojny." *Wrzesień 1939*. ('Polish War Plan.' "September 1939.") Edited by Bohdan Skaradzinski and Zdzisław Szpakowski. Warsaw: Więź, 1972.

_____. *Wojna polska 1939*. ("The Polish War 1939.") Poznań: Wydawnictwo Poznańskie, 1972.

Moravec, Frantisek. *Master of Spies*. New York: Doubleday & Company, 1975.

Namier, Lewis B. *Diplomatic Prelude, 1938-1939*. London: Macmillan & Co. Ltd., 1948.

_____. *Europe in Decay*. London: Macmillan & Co. LTD, 1950.

_____. *In the Nazi Era*. London: Macmillan & Co. LTD, 1952.

Nicolson, Harold. *Peace Making 1919*. New York: The Universal Library Grosset & Dunlap, 1965.

Noël, Leon. *Agresja niemiecka na Polske*. ("German Aggression on Poland.") Edited by Stanislaw Zabiello. Warsaw: PAX, 1966.

Nowak, C.M. *Czechoslovak-Polish Relations, 1918-1939: A Selected and Annotated Bibliography*. Stanford, California: Hoover Institution Press, 1976.

Ordon, Stanisław. *Wojna obronna Polski w 1939 roku na wybrzeżu i morzu w świetle prawa międzynarodowego.* ("Poland's War of Defense in 1939 on the Coast and at Sea in the Light of International Law.") Wrocław: Ossolineum, 1974.

Perman, D. *The Shaping of the Czechoslovak State.* Leiden: E.J. Brill, 1962.

Piłsudski, Józef. *Year 1920.* New York: Piłsudski Institute of America, 1972.

Pobóg-Malinowski, Władysław. *Najnowsza historia polityczna Polski, 1864-1945.* ("The Modern History of Poland, 1864-1945.") Vol. II London: B. Swiderski, 1967. Vol. III. London: Privately printed, 1960.

Polonsky, Antony. *Politics in Independent Poland 1921-1939.* Oxford: The Clarendon Press, 1972.

Pułaski, Michał. *Stosunki dyplomatyczne polsko-czechosłowacko-niemieckie od roku 1933 do wiosny 1938.* ("Polish-Czechoslovak-German Diplomatic Relations from 1933 to Spring 1938.") Poznań: Wydawnictwo Poznańskie, 1967.

Raczyński, Edward. *In Allied London.* London: Weidenfeld, 1976.

Raina, Peter. *Stosunki polsko-niemieckie 1937-1939.* ("Polish-German Relations 1937-1939.") London: Oficyna Poetów i Malarzy, 1975.

Reile, O. *Geheime Ostfront, Die Deutsche Abwehr in Osten 1921-1945.* Munich, 1963.

Ripka, H. *Munich, Before and After.* Gollancz, 1939.

Robertson, Esmonde M., ed. *The Origins of the Second World War.* New York: St. Martin's, 1972.

Roos, Hans. *A History of Modern Poland.* New York: Alfred A. Knopf, 1966.

Rose, William J. *The Drama of Upper Silesia.* Brattleboro: Stephen Daye Press, 1935.

Rothschild, Joseph. *Piłsudski's Coup d'Etat.* New York: Columbia University Press, 1966.

Rzepniewski, Andrzej. *Obrona wybrzeża w 1939 r.* ("Defense of the Coast in 1939.") Warsaw: MON, 1970.

Sabaliunas, Leonas. *Lithuania in Crisis: Nationalism to Communism 1939-1940.* Bloomington: Indiana University Press, 1972.

Schmitt, Bernadotte E. *Poland.* Berkeley: University of California Press, 1945.

Schuschnigg, Kurt von. *Austrian Requiem.* New York, 1946.

Seton-Watson, Hugh. *Eastern Europe between the Wars 1918-1941.* Cambridge, Massachusetts: Cambridge University Press, 1945.

Shellenberg, Walter. *The Labyrinth.* New York, 1956.

Sierpowski, Stanisław. *Stosunki polsko-włoskie w latach 1918-1940.*

("Polish-Italian Relations 1918-1940.") Warsaw: Państwowe Wydawnictwo Naukowe, 1975.

Sokolnicki, Michał. *Rok czternasty.* ("The Fourteenth Year.") London: Gryf Publications Ltd., 1961.

Staniewicz, Restytut W. "Elementy polskich przygotowan do wojny z Niemcami 1933-1939." *Wrzesień 1939.* ('Elements of Polish Preparedness for War with Germany 1933-1939.' "September 1939.") Edited by Bohdan Skaradziński and Zdzisław Szpakowski. Warsaw: Wieź, 1972.

Stanisławska, Stefania. *Polska a Monachium.* ("Poland and Munich.") Warsaw: Kziążka i Wiedza, 1967.

——————. *Wielka i mała polityka Józefa Becka.* ("Great and Small Politics of Józef Beck.") Warsaw: Polski Instytut Spraw Międzynarodowych, 1962.

Starzeński, Paweł. *3 lata z Beckiem.* ("3 Years with Beck.") London: Polska Fundacja Kulturalna, 1972.

Stercho, Peter. *Diplomacy of Double Morality.* New York: Carpathian Research Center, 1971.

Stevenson, William. *A Man Called Intrepid.* New York: Harcourt Brace Jovanovich, 1976.

Strang, Lord. *At Home and Abroad.* London: Deutsch, 1956.

Sworakowski, Witold. *Polacy na Slasku za Olza.* ("Poles beyond the Silesian Trans-Olza.") Warsaw: Instytut Badań Spraw Narodowosciowych, 1937.

Szefer, Andrzej. "Mniejszość niemiecka w Polsce w służbie V Kolumny hitlerowskiej." ("The German Minority in Poland in Service to the German Nazi V Column.") *Irredenta niemiecka w Europie środkowej i południowowschodniej przed II wojną światową.* ("German Irredentism in Central and South-Eastern Europe before the II World War.") Edited by Henryk Batowski. Cracow: Państwowe Wydawnictwo Naukowe, 1971.

Szembek, Jan. *Diariusz i teki.* ("Diary and Papers.") Edited by Tytus Komarnicki. Volumes I, II. London: Polish Research Centre, 1964-65. Volumes III, IV. London: Polish Institute and Sikorski Museum, 1969-72.

Szklarska-Lohmannowa, Alina. *Polsko-czechosłowackie stosunki dyplomatyczne 1918-1925.* ("Polish-Czechoslovak Diplomatic Relations 1918-1925.") Warsaw: Polska Akademia Nauk, 1967.

Szymański, Antoni. *Zły sąsiad.* ("Bad Neighbor.") London: Veritas, n.d.

Taylor, A.J.P. *Origins of the Second World War.* New York: Atheneum, 1962.

Templewood, Viscount. *Nine Troubled Years.* London: Collins St James's Place, 1954.

The German Fifth Column in Poland. London: Hutchinson & Co. Ltd., n.d.

Torzecki, Ryszard. *Kwestia ukraińska w polityce III Rzeszy 1933-1945.* ("The Ukrainian Question in the Politics of III Reich 1933-1945.") Warsaw: Książka i Wiedza, 1972.

Turlejska, Maria. *Rok przed klęską.* ("The Year before the Defeat.") Warsaw: Wiedza Powszechna, 1962.

Vansittart, Lord. *The Mist Procession.* London: Hutchinson, 1958.

Vorman, N. von. *Der Feldzug 1939 in Polen.* Weissenburg, 1958.

Wagner, Dieter and Tomkowitz, Gerhard. *The Week after Hitler Seized Vienna.* New York: St. Martin's Press, 1972.

Wandycz, Piotr S. *France and Her Eastern Allies 1919-1925.* Minneapolis: The University of Minnesota Press, 1962.

——————. *Soviet-Polish Relations 1917-1921.* Cambridge, Massachusetts: Harvard University Press, 1969.

Wheeler-Bennett, John. *Munich.* New York: Duell, Sloan and Pearce, 1948.

Whiting, Charles. *The Spymasters.* New York: Saturday Review Press, 1976.

Winterbotham, F.W. *The Ultra Secret.* New York: Harper & Row, 1974.

Wiskemann, Elizabeth. *Czechs and Germans.* London: Oxford University Press, 1938.

Wojciechowski, Zygmunt, ed. *Poland's Place in Europe.* Poznań: Instytut Zachodni, 1947.

Wojciechowski, Marian. *Stosunki polsko-niemieckie 1933-1938.* ("Polish-German Relations 1933-1938.") Poznań: Instytut Zachodni, 1965.

Wrzesiński, Wojciech. *Polski ruch narodowy w Niemczech 1922-1939.* ("Polish National Movement in Germany 1922-1939.") Poznań: Wydawnictwo Poznańskie, 1970.

Wynot, Edward D., Jr. *Polish Politics in Transition.* Athens: The University of Georgia Press, 1974.

Żarnowski, Janusz. *Polska Partia Socjalistyczna w latach 1935-1939.* ("Polish Socialist Party 1935-1939.") Warsaw: Książka i Wiedza, 1965.

Zgorniak, Marian. *Wojskowe aspekty kryzysu czechosłowackiego 1938 roku.* ("Military Aspects of the 1938 Czechoslovak Crisis.") Cracow: Uniwersytet Jagiellonski, 1966.

Periodicals

Batowski, Henryk. "Rumuńska podróż Becka w październiku 1938 roku." ("Beck's Trip to Rumania in October 1938.") *Kwartalnik Historyczny* Vol. LXV, No. 2 (1958).

Budurowycz, Bohdan B. "Poland and Hitler's Offers of Alliance." *The Polish Review,* Vol. III, No. 4 (Autumn, 1958).

Dopierała, Bogdan. "Problemy syntezy dziejów polityki morskiej II Rzeczypospolitej." ("The Synthesis of Maritime Problems of the II Polish Republic.") *Dzieje Najnowsze,* Vol. VI, No. 3.

Gondek, Leszek. "Antyhitlerowska współpraca Oddziału II Sztabu Głównego WP z wywiadami innych państw." ("Anti-Hitler Polish Intelligence Cooperation with Other Countries.") *Przegląd Zachodni*, Vol. XXXI, No. 1 (1975).

Gromada, Thaddeus. "Piłsudski and the Slovak Autonomists." *Slavic Review*, Vol. XXVIII, No. 3 (1969).

──────────. "The Slovaks and the Failure of Beck's 'Third Europe' Scheme." *Essays on Poland's Foreign Policy 1918-1939*, Piłsudski Institute of America (1970).

Kosiński, Leszek A. "Secret German War-Sources for Population Study of East Central Europe and Soviet Union." *East European Quarterly*, Vol. X, No. 1 (Spring 1976).

Kozaczuk, Władysław. "Enigma." *Stolica*, Vol. XXIX, Nos. 1409-1440 (1974-1975).

Kozeński, Jerzy. "Kwestia słowacka w polityce Trzeciej Rzeszy." ("The Slovak Question in the Politics of the Third Reich.") *Studia z Dziejów ZSRR i Europy Srodkowej*, Vol. X.

──────────. "The Nazi Subjugation of Slovakia, March-September 1939." *Polish Western Affairs*, Vol. XII (1971).

Kuplinski, Jerzy. "Z dziejów wychodźstwa czechosłowackiego w Polsce po zaborze Czechosłowacji w roku 1939." ("The Chronicle of Czechoslovak Refugees in 1939 Poland after the Fall of Czechoslovakia.") *Studia z Dziejów ZSRR i Europy Srodkowej* Vol. X (1974).

Magocsi, Paul R. "The Ruthenian Decision to Unite with Czechoslovakia." *Slavic Review*, Vol. XXXIV (June 1975).

Papée, Kazimierz. "Kartki z pamiętnika." ("Cards from Memoirs.") *Wiadomości*, No. 834 (London, 1962).

Podkowiński, Marian. "Hasło: 'Konserwy'," ("Callword: 'Canned Goods'.") *Perspektywy*, Vol. VII, No. 35 (August 1975).

Roman, Eric. "Munich and Hungary: An Overview of Hungarian Diplomacy during the Sudeten Crisis." *East European Quarterly*, Vol. VIII, No. 1 (March 1974).

Sontag, R.J. "The Last Months of Peace, 1939." *Foreign Affairs* (April 1957).

Sprawy Międzynarodowe, VII and VIII (July-August, 1958).

Stasierski, Kazimierz. "Polscy uchodźcy na Węgrzech w latach 1939-1945." ("Polish Refugees in Hungary 1939-1945.") *Przegląd Historyczny*, Vol. LII, No. 2 (1961).

Steblik, Władysław. "Niemiecki napad na Przełecz Jabłonkówska w nocy z 25 na 26.8.1939 r." ("German Attack on Jabłonków Pass the Night of 25-26 August 1939.") *Wojskowy Przegląd Historyczny*, No. 4 (1965).

Strzelecki, Leon. "Gry wojenne Marszałka Piłsudskiego." ("Marshal Piłsudski's War Games.") *Niepodległość*, Vol. VII (1962).

Szumowski, Tadeusz. "Legia Czechów i Słowaków." ("Czech and Slovak Legion.") *Kierunki*, No. 20 (1968).

Taborsky, Edward. "The Triumph and Disaster of Eduard Benes." *Foreign Affairs*, Vol. XXXVI, No. 4 (July 1958).

Woytak, Richard A. "Wywiad z litewskim Wodzem Naczelnym gen. Stasys'em Rastikis'em." ("Interview with the Lithuanian Commander and Chief General Stasys Rastikis.") *Zeszyty Historyczne*, Vol. 261, No. 35 (1976).

Żeleński, Władysław. "Zabójstwo Ministra Pierackiego." ("Assassination of Minister Pieracki.") *Zeszyty Historyczne*, Vol. 232, No. 25 (1973).

Zgórniak, Marian. "'Fall Otto' i kryzys marcowy 1938 r." ("'Fall Otto' and the March 1938 Crisis.") *Wojskowy Przeglad Historyczny*, Vol. 71, No. 4 (1974).

Newspapers

Dziennik Polski (London), 1970-1976.
Gazeta Polska (Warsaw), 1938-1939.
Sprawy Narodowościowe (Warsaw), 1938-1939.
The New York Times, 1938-1939.

INDEX

Altentenburg, Gunther, head of the Political Division German For. Ministry March 1939: 71

Anglo-Polish Agreement (August 25, 1939): 84

Anschluss, chap. 1; *see also* Austria

Anti-Comintern Pact, 63, 66, 68

Arlet, Wiesław, 92

Austria: mobilisation of, 11; Polish intelligence in 12-13; German occupation March 12, 1938, plebiscite March 13, 14

AVA, 9

Bartik, Joseph, Maj.: proposal on Czech-Polish intelligence exchange, 83-84

Beck, Józef (1894-1944), Polish For. Minister Nov. 1932 to Sept. 1939: 2, on Danzig, 6; to Kánya on Czechoslovakia, 10-11; with Göring Feb. 23, 1938, 11-12; with Mussolini, 15; answer to Anglo-French demarches, 27-28; demands equal treatment of Polish minority in Czech., 33; answers Soviet protest on troop concentration, 34-35; on Munich Conference, 38-39; at Warsaw Castle Sept. 30, 1938, 40-41; Kánya to, on Trans-Olza, 51; on Hungary, 54-55; conference of his ministers, 59; rejection of Ribbentrop proposals on Danzig, 62; to Szembek on Hungary, von Moltke on Carpatho-Ukraine, 63; instructions to Lipski

Dec. 1938, 65; conversations with Hitler and Ribbentrop Jan. 5-6, 1939, 67-68; Ribbentrop visit, agreement on Danzig Jan. 25-27, 68-69; Ciano-Beck meeting Feb. 25 to March 3, 71; on Danzig March 24, 81; reply to Hitler, London visit of, 82; Polish-Anglo agreement April 6, 84

Beck, Ludwig, Gen.: 12-13

Beneš, Edward (1884-1948), For. Minister of Czechoslovakia 1918-35, President 1935-38, 1939-48; 19, concessions to Sudeten German Party, 30; appeal to USSR, 31; letter to Moscicki, 35-36; on Teschen and Frystadt, 36-37; accepts Munich, 38; accepts Polish ultimatum, 40; Czech-Polish intelligence exchange, 83; Prchala under orders of, 88

Bertrand, Major: with *section d'examin*, 88; *Enigma* collaboration, 89

Bethlen, Istvan, Count: to Orłowski, 57

Biddle, Drexel J. (1891-1961), U.S. Ambassador in Warsaw 1937-39; for Roosevelt, 41

Bonnet, Georges (1883-1973), French For. Minister April 1938 to Sept. 1939: to Łukasiewicz on Czech., 27; proposal to Beck May 22, 1938, 29-30; to Łukasiewicz Sept. 22, 33

aid to *Sitch* forces, 70; Hitler to Brauchitsch on Danzig, 81; Hitler's war directive, 82-3; agents in Danzig, 85; fortification of Danzig by, 91

Weizacker, Ernst, von, Baron (1882-1951), Acting Director Polical Department, German For. Ministry 1936-38, Secretary of State 1938-43: discussion of Polish claims in Czechoslovakia, 40; telegram to Khust, 72

Werth, Henrik, Gen., Chief of the Hungarian General Staff, 71

Westerplatte, *see* Danzig

Wilson, Horace, Sir, (1882), chief industrial advisor to the British govt., 1930-39, Treasury, advisor to N. Chamberlin: in laison to Hitler, 37

Wicher, 8, 10

Woermann, Ernst, director of the political division, German For. Ministry, 61

Wózek, 22

Wraga-Niezbrzycki, Jerzey, head of the eastern division, Polish Intelligence, 77

Wrzeszczynski, Polish attache in Moscow, 88

Żychoń, Jan, Maj., Chief of Intelligence, Center No. 3, 32, 77

Zygalski, Henryk, 8

EAST EUROPEAN MONOGRAPHS

The *East European Monographs* comprise scholarly books on the history and civilization of Eastern Europe. They are published by the *East European Quarterly* in the belief that these studies contribute substantially to the knowledge of the area and serve to stimulate scholarship and research.

1. *Political Ideas and the Enlightenment in the Romanian Principalities, 1750–1831.* By Vlad Georgescu. 1971.
2. *America, Italy and the Birth of Yugoslavia, 1917–1919.* By Dragan R. Zivojinovic. 1972.
3. *Jewish Nobles and Geniuses in Modern Hungary.* By William O. McCagg, Jr. 1972.
4. *Mixail Soloxov in Yugoslavia: Reception and Literary Impact.* By Robert F. Price. 1973.
5. *The Historical and National Thought of Nicolae Iorga.* By William O. Oldson. 1973.
6. *Guide to Polish Libraries and Archives.* By Richard C. Lewanski. 1974.
7. *Vienna Broadcasts to Slovakia, 1938–1939: A Case Study in Subversion.* By Henry Delfiner. 1974.
8. *The 1917 Revolution in Latvia.* By Andrew Ezergailis. 1974.
9. *The Ukraine in the United Nations Organization: A Study in Soviet Foreign Policy. 1944–1950.* By Konstantin Sawczuk. 1975.
10. *The Bosnian Church: A New Interpretation.* By John V. A. Fine, Jr., 1975.
11. *Intellectual and Social Developments in the Habsburg Empire from Maria Theresa to World War I.* Edited by Stanley B. Winters and Joseph Held. 1975.
12. *Ljudevit Gaj and the Illyrian Movement.* By Elinor Murray Despalatovic. 1975.
13. *Tolerance and Movements of Religious Dissent in Eastern Europe.* Edited by Bela K. Kiraly. 1975.
14. *The Parish Republic: Hlinka's Slovak People's Party, 1939–1945.* By Yeshayahu Jelinek. 1976.
15. *The Russian Annexation of Bessarabia, 1774–1828.* By George F. Jewsbury. 1976.
16. *Modern Hungarian Historiography.* By Steven Bela Vardy. 1976.
17. *Values and Community in Multi-National Yugoslavia.* By Gary K. Bertsch. 1976.
18. *The Greek Socialist Movement and the First World War: the Road to Unity.* By George B. Leon. 1976.
19. *The Radical Left in the Hungarian Revolution of 1848.* By Laszlo Deme. 1976.

20. *Hungary between Wilson and Lenin: The Hungarian Revolution of 1918–1919 and the Big Three.* By Peter Pastor. 1976.
21. *The Crises of France's East-Central European Diplomacy, 1933–1938.* By Anthony J. Komjathy. 1976.
22. *Polish Politics and National Reform, 1775–1788.* By Daniel Stone. 1976.
23. *The Habsburg Empire in World War I.* Robert A. Kann, Bela K. Kiraly, and Paula S. Fichtner, eds. 1977.
24. *The Slovenes and Yugoslavism, 1890–1914.* By Carole Rogel. 1977.
25. *German-Hungarian Relations and the Swabian Problem.* By Thomas Spira. 1977.
26. *The Metamorphosis of a Social Class in Hungary During the Reign of Young Franz Joseph.* By Peter I. Hidas. 1977.
27. *Tax Reform in Eighteenth Century Lombardy.* By Daniel M. Klang. 1977.
28. *Tradition versus Revolution: Russia and the Balkans in 1917.* By Robert H. Johnston. 1977.
29. *Winter into Spring: The Czechoslovak Press and the Reform Movement 1963–1968.* By Frank L. Kaplan. 1977.
30. *The Catholic Church and the Soviet Government, 1939–1949.* By Dennis J. Dunn. 1977.
31. *The Hungarian Labor Service System, 1939–1945.* By Randolph L. Braham. 1977.
32. *Consciousness and History: Nationalist Critics of Greek Society 1897–1914.* By Gerasimos Augustinos. 1977.
33. *Emigration in Polish Social and Political Thought, 1870–1914.* By Benjamin P. Murdzek. 1977.
34. *Serbian Poetry and Milutin Bojic.* By Mihailo Dordevic. 1977.
35. *The Baranya Dispute: Diplomacy in the Vortex of Ideologies, 1918–1921.* By Leslie C. Tihany. 1978.
36. *The United States in Prague, 1945–1948.* By Walter Ullmann. 1978.
37. *Rush to the Alps: The Evolution of Vacationing in Switzerland.* By Paul P. Bernard. 1978.
38. *Transportation in Eastern Europe: Empirical Findings.* By Bogdan Mieczkowski. 1978.
39. *The Polish Underground State: A Guide to the Underground, 1939–1945.* By Stefan Korbonski. 1978.
40. *The Hungarian Revolution of 1956 in Retrospect.* Edited by Bela K. Kiraly and Paul Jonas. 1978.
41. *Boleslaw Limanowski (1835–1935): A Study in Socialism and Nationalism.* By Kazimiera Janina Cottam. 1978.
42. *The Lingering Shadow of Nazism: The Austrian Independent Party Movement Since 1945.* By Max E. Riedlsperger. 1978.
43. *The Catholic Church, Dissent and Nationality in Soviet Lithuania.* By V. Stanley Vardys. 1978.

44. *The Development of Parliamentary Government in Serbia.* By Alex N. Dragnich. 1978.
45. *Divide and Conquer: German Efforts to Conclude a Separate Peace. 1914-1918.* By L. L. Farrar, Jr. 1978.
46. *The Prague Slav Congress of 1848.* By Lawrence D. Orton. 1978.
47. *The Nobility and the Making of the Hussite Revolution.* By John M. Klassen. 1978.
48. *The Cultural Limits of Revolutionary Politics: Change and Continuity in Socialist Czechoslovakia.* By David W. Paul. 1979.
49. *On the Border of War and Peace: Polish Intelligence and Diplomacy in 1937-1939 and the Origins of the Ultra Secret.* By Richard A. Woytak. 1979.